Praise for W
Don't Like Y

"I deeply understand the pain of not liking parts of my own story. Yet time and again, I've seen God restore and redeem my life even when it doesn't end up the way I would have chosen. The stories and hope within the pages of *When You Don't Like Your Story* are a gift to the world, and I'm grateful my friend Sharon has written this treasure for us all!"

—LYSA TERKEURST, #1 *NEW YORK TIMES* BESTSELLING
AUTHOR AND PRESIDENT OF PROVERBS 31 MINISTRIES

"If we're being honest, we all have parts of our story that we don't like, that we don't want, and corners of darkness that if we knew were coming would cause us to back away slowly, then turn and run as fast as we can. In *When You Don't Like Your Story* Sharon so graciously and practically illuminates how it's God's specialty to use our darkest days and turn them from trash into triumph. This book will invite you to look at your story with fresh eyes and walk in the freedom that comes from trusting God with every page."

—JENNIE LUSKO, LEAD PASTOR OF FRESH LIFE
CHURCH AND BESTSELLING AUTHOR

"Sharon Jaynes knows how to offer kind and wise encouragement for those times when life brings an unexpected turn or a painful circumstance. With grace and gentleness, she points us to the certainty of divine providence as our source of hope and peace."

—BOB LEPINE, COHOST OF *FAMILYLIFE TODAY*

"If you are living in the middle chapter of a painful story right now, I cannot recommend this book enough. So many of us attempt to wrap our heads around God's goodness and sovereignty, while our hearts continue to take a licking. Sharon Jaynes's *When You Don't Like Your Story* is the balm you need to heal the hurts and the courage to continue. This literary journey will give you the courage to persevere in your own journey."

—WENDY SPEAKE, AUTHOR OF *THE 40-DAY SOCIAL MEDIA FAST*, *THE 40-DAY SUGAR FAST*, AND COAUTHOR OF *TRIGGERS*

"Sharon's introductory words gripped my heart and held it to the last page. *When You Don't Like Your Story* will help you see that no matter who you are, what you have done, or what has been done to you, the world needs to hear your story of redemption, forgiveness, surrender, and grace. This book will not only help you see why your story matters but will also help you tell it."

—PAT LAYTON, AUTHOR, *LIFE UNSTUCK: FINDING PEACE WITH YOUR PAST, PURPOSE IN YOUR PRESENT, AND PASSION FOR YOUR FUTURE*

"If your story isn't turning out the way you planned, Sharon Jaynes will help you have hope for the future, strength for your current circumstances, and peace even when you don't understand. This book is a powerful and encouraging reminder of what's true no matter what: the Author of your life is good, you are loved, and He alone holds the pen that gets to write 'The End.'"

—HOLLEY GERTH, LIFE COACH AND BESTSELLING AUTHOR OF *THE POWERFUL PURPOSE OF INTROVERTS: WHY THE WORLD NEEDS YOU TO BE YOU*

"Most of us have an imperfect life story but too often we stay stuck, waiting for the 'happily-ever-after' to magically happen to us. But every epic narrative has a heroic guide that helps lead the characters to their victory! Sharon Jaynes is that wise, trusted, and experienced mentor who God *will use* to transform your tale into triumph. *Your Worst Chapters CAN Become*

Your Greatest Victories. I know, because God did it for me, for Sharon, and is waiting to give you a life story that will be used to bless and build others too. This book is the key to your future."

—PAM FARREL, AUTHOR OF BESTSELLING *MEN ARE LIKE WAFFLES, WOMEN ARE LIKE SPAGHETTI*

"For every season of life you wish you could forget, every choice you carry in secret shame and the anger that burns for what's been done to you, Sharon Jaynes has a message: God wastes nothing! In *When You Don't Like Your Story*, Sharon takes you on a journey through personal and biblical stories that will show you how God is using everything that has happened to you to prepare you for an extraordinary destiny! This is a book to read and reread as God's Truth poured through the pages will restore your heart for what is ahead."

—GLYNNIS WHITWER, EXECUTIVE DIRECTOR OF COMMUNICATONS, PROVERBS 31 MINISTRIES

"Few things are as lonely as an unexpected story. Faced with a reality that doesn't look at all like you imagined, it's oh-so-easy to slip into a pit of regret and despair. *Is there any hope? Will I ever feel real joy again?* With both truth and grace, Sharon Jaynes offers you the comfort of her presence and experience, gently reminding you that in even the hardest of stories, there is still Hope. And His name is Jesus."

—MICHELE CUSHATT, AUTHOR OF *RELENTLESS: THE UNSHAKEABLE PRESENCE OF A GOD WHO NEVER LEAVES*

"Almost all of us have parts to our story we would like to erase. I know I've made mistakes, said wrong things, and taken some wrong turns that I only wish I could undo. This is why I am thankful for Sharon Jaynes's new book *When You Don't Like Your Story*. I am reminded that God is always working, even in hard-to-make-sense-of histories. Grabbing hold of the truths within these pages has encouraged me to give the broken pieces of my life to God and watch Him do amazing things."

—KELLY BALARIE, AUTHOR OF *REST NOW: 7 WAYS TO SAY NO, SET BOUNDARIES, AND SEIZE JOY*

"*When You Don't Like Your Story* is a powerful reminder that God's redemptive grace can rewrite the most tragic of tales—including yours. God invites each of us beyond our broken to His beauty. These pages give clear, biblical direction to help you move forward and step into a better story."

—GWEN SMITH, HOST OF THE *GRACEOLOGIE* PODCAST,
AUTHOR OF *I WANT IT ALL* AND *BROKEN INTO BEAUTIFUL*

WHEN YOU
DON'T
LIKE YOUR
STORY

ALSO BY SHARON JAYNES

The Power of a Woman's Words: How the Words
You Speak Shape the Lives of Others
Enough: Silencing the Lies That Steal Your Confidence
Take Hold of the Faith You Long For: Let
Go, Move Forward, Live Bold
A Sudden Glory: God's Response to Your Ache for Something More
Knowing God by Name
Trusting God
Becoming a Woman Who Listens to God
Building an Effective Women's Ministry

BOOKS ON MARRIAGE AND FAMILY
Lovestruck: Discovering God's Design for
Romance, Marriage, and Sexual Intimacy
Praying for Your Husband from Head to Toe:
A Scriptural Guide to Daily Prayer
A 14-Day Romance Challenge
Becoming the Woman of His Dreams: Seven
Qualities Every Man Longs For
Being a Great Mom, Raising Great Kids

WHEN YOU
DON'T
LIKE YOUR
STORY

*What If Your Worst Chapters Could
Become Your Greatest Victories?*

SHARON JAYNES

NELSON
BOOKS

An Imprint of Thomas Nelson

Published in Nashville, Tennessee, by Nelson Books, an imprint of Thomas Nelson. Nelson Books and Thomas Nelson are registered trademarks of HarperCollins Christian Publishing, Inc.

Thomas Nelson titles may be purchased in bulk for educational, business, fund-raising, or sales promotional use. For information, please e-mail SpecialMarkets@ThomasNelson.com.

Unless otherwise noted, Scripture quotations are taken from the Holy Bible, New International Version®, NIV®. Copyright © 1973, 1978, 1984, 2011 by Biblica, Inc.® Used by permission of Zondervan. All rights reserved worldwide. www.Zondervan.com. The "NIV" and "New International Version" are trademarks registered in the United States Patent and Trademark Office by Biblica, Inc.® Scripture quotations marked AMPC are taken from the *Amplified® Bible, Classic Edition,* Copyright © 1954, 1958, 1962, 1964, 1965, 1987, by the Lockman Foundation. Used by permission (www.Lockman.org.) All rights reserved. Scripture quotations marked ESV are from the ESV® Bible (The Holy Bible, English Standard Version®). Copyright © 2001 by Crossway, a publishing ministry of Good News Publishers. Used by permission. All rights reserved. Scripture quotations marked THE MESSAGE are from *The Message.* Copyright © by Eugene H. Peterson 1993, 1994, 1995, 1996, 2000, 2001, 2002. Used by permission of NavPress. All rights reserved. Represented by Tyndale House Publishers, Inc. Scripture quotations marked NET are from the NET Bible®. Copyright © 1996–2006 by Biblical Studies Press, L.L.C. http:// netbible.com. All rights reserved. Scripture quotations marked NLT are from the Holy Bible, New Living Translation. © 1996, 2004, 2007, 2013, 2015 by Tyndale House Foundation. Used by permission of Tyndale House Publishers, Inc., Carol Stream, Illinois 60188. All rights reserved. Scripture quotations marked CSB are taken from the *Christian Standard Bible®,* Copyright © 2017 by Holman Bible Publishers. Used by permission. *Christian Standard Bible®* and CSB® are federally registered trademarks of Holman Bible Publishers.

Any Internet addresses, phone numbers, or company or product information printed in this book are offered as a resource and are not intended in any way to be or to imply an endorsement by Thomas Nelson, nor does Thomas Nelson vouch for the existence, content, or services of these sites, phone numbers, companies, or products beyond the life of this book.

ISBN 978-1-4002-0970-5 (TP)   ISBN 978-1-4002-0971-2 (eBook)

Library of Congress Cataloging-in-Publication Data

Names: Jaynes, Sharon, author.
Title: When you don't like your story : what if your worst chapters could be your greatest victories? / Sharon Jaynes.
Description: Nashville : Nelson Books, 2020. | Includes bibliographical references. | Summary: "Bestselling author, cofounder of Girlfriends in God, and writer for Proverbs 31 Ministries Sharon Jaynes reveals the secret to living a better story: understanding that the worst parts of our past are the very things God uses most"-- Provided by publisher.
Identifiers: LCCN 2020021814 | ISBN 9781400209705 | ISBN 9781400209712 (epub)
Subjects: LCSH: Self-actualization (Psychology)--Religious aspects--Christianity. | Success--Religious aspects--Christianity. | Regret--Religious aspects--Christianity. | Providence and government of God--Christianity. | Trust in God--Christianity.
Classification: LCC BV4598.2 .J395 2020 | DDC 248.4--dc23 LC record available at https://lccn.loc. gov/2020021814

Printed in the United States of America
HB 02.20.2024

To Linda Butler
For shared stories and shared lives
Forever friends

Contents

Chapter One

May I Please Have a
Different Story?

Your life story is a biography of wisdom and grace
written by Another. Every twist of the plot is for the
best. Every turn he writes into your story is right.
Every new character or unexpected event is a tool of
his grace. Each new chapter advances his purpose.

—Paul Tripp, *You Are Not the Author of Your Story*

Mommy, tell me a story."

That was a common request when my son was a little guy. Whether riding in the car, getting a haircut, or being tucked in at bedtime, Steven loved for me to tell him a story. The one requirement for my made-up tales was that Steven had to give me the first line. "Okay, buddy," I'd say, "what's the first sentence?"

"Once upon a time there was a leaf . . ."

"Once upon a time there was a snail . . ."

"Once upon a time there was a tree . . ."

"Once upon a time there was a dragon . . ."

And so, the tale would begin.

Everybody loves a good story, but not everybody loves their own story. Mistakes pile high like weeks-old laundry. Shame whispers, "If they only knew." Tear-stained pages warp and cause the volume to fall open to unwanted pages. Dog-eared corners mark traumatic happenings we keep going back to in order to make sense of it all. Some pages have spots worn thin from rubbing a mental eraser over words that won't go away. Lines we've tried to cross out instead stand out and taunt us. We've all got them—unwanted pages. *Yes, I'd like a different story, please.*

For most of us, it is not the whole of our stories that we don't like, but just certain parts. Our tragedies, traumas, and too-dark-to-tell memories may be different, but the pain is the same.

A husband left.
A boyfriend cheated.
A friend betrayed.
A parent abused.
A boss misused.
A disease ravished.
A steering wheel jerked.
A gunshot fired.
A child died.

I don't know the difficulties you've been through, but I do know your story didn't end there. There is more to be written, and God is even now dipping his pen into the inkwell of wholeness, writing your story and mine into his larger story. God turns broken stories into beautiful prose and unwanted pages into stunning narratives of victory. That's not just a promise; it's a bedrock truth—one I know from personal experience.

HOPE IN THE HIDING PLACE

I grew up in eastern North Carolina in a nice neighborhood and a nice house. But much of what went on behind the door of our ranch-style house was anything but nice.

My father didn't drink every day, but when he did drink, he got drunk. When he got drunk, he grew violent. Yelling and violent outbursts were common occurrences in our home. My parents fought both verbally and physically in front of my brother and me, and we lived much of our lives in fear. I saw many things a little girl should never see and heard words a little girl should never hear. I didn't know what some of the words meant, but I knew how they made me feel.

God turns broken stories into beautiful prose and unwanted pages into stunning narratives of victory.

On many nights, I went to bed, pulled up the covers around my quivering chin, and prayed I would quickly fall asleep to escape the yelling in the next room. On my dresser, I had a musical jewelry box with a ballerina that popped up when the lid opened. Many nights, I tiptoed over to the jewelry box, turned the wind-up key in the back, and opened the lid in hopes the tinkling music would drown out the fighting in the next room.

The builders who constructed our house had neglected to put a wall on the far end of my closet, between where my closet stopped and my brother's closet began. Some nights, I hid in that secret passageway. Other nights, I crawled through the tunnel to hide in my brother's room.

The worst nights were when my momma ran into my room and yelled at Daddy, "Do it in front of her! I want her to see you do it!" My mom wanted me to hate my dad, and this was her way of exposing the monster within. The next morning, I'd wake up to find my mom covered with cuts and bruises, the furniture scattered like Tinkertoys, and my dad crying and begging forgiveness, swearing it would never happen again. But it always did.

I felt that I was always in the way, a poor excuse for a daughter, and a burden to be tolerated rather than a child to be loved. If your own parents don't love you, then who in the world would? I concluded I wasn't smart enough, pretty enough, or good enough—just not enough, period. Insecurity, inadequacy, and inferiority dogged me, shouting accusations and heaping condemnation on my little-girl soul.

Now that I'm an adult, I understand that the story of my life isn't a stand-alone volume but one in a series. My parents both had their own stories. Mom was the middle child in a slew of twelve kids raised on a farm in one of the poorest counties of North Carolina. My father's dad died when he was six. Dad and his five siblings were raised by a single mom on the heels of the Depression. They had their own childhood disappointments, struggles, and heartaches scribbled across the pages of their lives. And when these two teenagers married, their hardscrabble stories got only harder as they tried to make a life together. I'm sure they loved me the best they knew how, but neither of them knew how to make a family work.

That's where our family story began, but God didn't leave us in that sorry state. I can't wait to tell you what happened. For now, know that there are some parts of my story I spent many years desperately wishing I could rip from the narrative. But here's what I've discovered: the parts of my story I wish had been edited out have become the ones God has highlighted as his most amazing work in my life.

We cannot delete, discard, or amend the past, but we can repurpose and reclaim the present. And when we do, we get something better than we ever imagined—a masterful work of God's redemption and grace to share with the world, a world that needs to hear the story that only we can tell.

SCARS OF GRACE AND REMEMBRANCE

Have you ever heard of the art of Kintsugi? It offers one of the most beautiful metaphors I know for what God does when he makes a masterwork of redemption from our stories. Kintsugi is the centuries-old Japanese art of fixing broken pottery with resin-dusted precious metals, such as gold, silver, or platinum. When the piece is mended, it becomes a work of art with shimmering veins connecting the broken shards. The art form of Kintsugi celebrates seeing beauty in the flawed or imperfect. The golden "scars" convey that broken and repaired objects are not something to hide, but to display with pride. In the end, the pottery is more valuable with the gold inlay filling the cracks than it was in its original state.

I thought about Kintsugi when I looked down at the young man's wrist and saw them—scars. It was hard to believe that just fifteen years earlier, this laughing man now beating my socks off at Gin Rummy had been lying in a hospital bed after attempting to take his own life. And yet, here he was—healthy and whole. Redemption at its best.

But redemption was the farthest thing from my mind when it happened. At the time, it seemed as if God had hijacked his happiness and flown him in a nosedive to lands unknown. It was so hard to watch it all unfold. *How could you?* I cried out to God. *Why would you?* I questioned. *You could have stopped this!* I accused. *Where are you?*

And yet, fifteen years later, I could see the faint reminders—the golden veins filling the cracks in the form of two scars. They were slight, but present. A reminder of how God had used his grace to fill the broken places and make the young man's life a showcase of redemption.

Do I wish the scars weren't part of this young man's story? Absolutely. But do I wish the scars were gone? Absolutely not. Does he? Not a chance. They represent the worst part of his story that God has used for the best parts of his redemption. God has used every tear shed to make the young man's compassion for others run deep and his knowledge of redemption concrete. God has used it all. Every crack of the broken pottery. Every shard. Every chip. Every slip.

Yes, there are great possibilities when we refuse to stop in the middle of a story and determine to keep moving forward with the flow of God's pen. We have great potential when we do not allow our present circumstances to determine our future destiny.

THE WHOLE STORY

I think we've all looked at our lives and wanted to rip a few pages from the narrative. But it's difficult to understand a story if there are missing chapters. Each chapter helps explain why characters are the way they are—why you and I are the way we are. We can't tear out a page or skip a chapter and still make sense of our story. But we can learn to embrace the story we were given and to trust God to keep writing our story into his.

I wouldn't have written my childhood story the way it now appears on the page. Instead, I would have had a daddy who loved me, a momma who cherished me, and a big brother who was my best friend forever. We would have spent holidays eating turkey, weekends playing board games, and quiet moments before bed saying goodnight prayers. But that's not the story I got.

I would have had a passel of children, a calendar overbooked with after-school activities, and walls full of picture-framed little ones all grown up. But that's not the story I got.

I would have had best friends who stayed friends for life, a happy-go-lucky personality that never struggled with discouragement, and all my books would have become *New York Times* bestsellers. But that's not the story I got.

What's the story you got? Whatever it is, I'm guessing there are pages you wish you could rip out of the narrative. I've never met a soul who didn't feel that way. But what I want to tell you is that the whole of it matters. Every crossed-out word. Every worn-thin erasure. Every ripped-out page. I believe that with my whole heart, because I believe you still *can* have a better story, even with the marred pages intact. You can change the ending of your story, even if it feels like you're trapped in a chapter that has come to a dead stop. There is a way to transform the worst parts of your story into a work of art. Your biggest mistakes have the potential to become God's greatest miracles.

Writing a better story is not an elaborate game of pretend. I'm not talking about dressing up an old story in new clothes and pretending it wasn't so bad. I'm not talking about packing it away somehow and acting like it never happened—or isn't happening still. No. What I'm talking about is how we can wrest redemption from the jaws of brokenness and then allow God to use it for good. It may be hard to believe that's possible if you're still living through a bad story, but don't give up hope. I have experienced it and witnessed it in the lives of others so many times—how God takes the hard things and uses them to showcase his mercy, grace, and forgiveness to create a new beginning. Yes, our worst scenes *can* become God's best. Our pain *can* become a portal of God's grace. Our ravaged pages *can* become God's redemptive masterpiece.

> *Our ravaged pages can become God's redemptive masterpiece.*

Artist and poet Terri St. Cloud once wrote, "She could never go back and make some of the details pretty. All she could do was move forward and make the whole beautiful."[1] That's what we're going to do—discover how to move forward and make the whole of our stories beautiful. If that seems like an impossibility at this point, I understand, but I promise you it is not. Together, we're going to discover the keys to having a better story, even with the parts we wish weren't there.

Chapter Two

Why Me? Why This? Why Now?

*What we see now is not the whole story. If we
could see what God sees and know what he
knows, our hearts would be at peace.*

—Nancy DeMoss Wolgemuth, *You Can
Trust God to Write Your Story*

My son, Steven, and I sat on the floor in his room playing a card game.
This summer was proving to be the best ever. Our golden retriever,
Ginger, had just delivered seven adorable puppies, Steven was enjoying
his sixth summer of life, and after four years of negative pregnancy
tests, God had surprised us with a new life growing inside my womb.

But as Steven and I sat cross-legged on the carpet, I felt a warm,
sticky sensation run down my leg. A trip to the bathroom confirmed
my greatest fears—I was bleeding. Later that afternoon, the doctor
voiced the weighty words, "There is no heartbeat."

What do you do when heartbreak slams into joy? When your soul
cracks open and there just aren't enough tears? When hurt steals your
hope and you want to give up on life? When deep soul lesions make a
mockery of your faith?

I wish I could tell you I left the doctor's office quoting Romans 8:28 about how "all things work together for good" (ESV). I wish I could tell you that I calmly accepted the loss of my baby with faith, trusting that even this was somehow part of God's plan. I wish I could tell you I spent the rest of the day singing "It Is Well with My Soul." But I didn't do any of those things.

I went home, crawled in bed, and pulled the covers up over my empty womb and broken heart. I didn't want to talk to anyone, especially God. And what I did say to him wasn't very nice.

How could you do this to me? If this is how you treat those you love, then just forget it! You answered my prayer only to take it back! Why me? Why this? Why now?

After my tearful outburst, I gave God the silent treatment, as if I could somehow pay him back. I mourned for my child and felt the ache of empty arms. I never realized until then how desperately I could miss someone I had never met. But, oh, how I missed her. We never knew for sure, but in my heart, I felt that the baby had been a little girl.

God and I had a lover's quarrel that summer. Actually, I was the only one arguing. I felt betrayed by the one who was supposed to love me most. Pierced by the one who was supposed to protect my heart. And while I gave God the cold shoulder, his warm embrace refused to let me go. He stayed right by my side, waiting, wooing, and drawing my hurting heart back to him. God always wants to heal our broken places and fill our empty spaces. I can see that now, but I couldn't see it then. So, as God persisted, I resisted.

Author Ann Voskamp wrote, "I wonder . . . if the rent in the canvas of our life backdrop, the losses that puncture our world, our own emptiness, might actually become places to see. To see through to God."[1] I had been thrust into one of those rents, a see-through place, but until I opened my eyes, I would not see God through the loss of my child.

Holocaust survivor Corrie ten Boom often quoted her sister

Betsie's words, "There is no pit so deep, that God's love is not deeper still."[2] After a time, God's love lifted me from the muck and mire and set my feet upon the rock. But even rescue didn't come without struggle. Just as the biblical patriarch Jacob wrestled with God in his dark night of the soul, I wrestled with God to make sense of why bad things happen.

WHY DO BAD THINGS HAPPEN?

Before we delve into how to have a better story—how to transform our worst chapters into our greatest victories—we need to acknowledge the proverbial elephant in the room. Why are bad chapters part of our narratives in the first place? Why does a loving God allow such pain?

There's no easy answer to why bad things happen. But the Bible does acknowledge at least three reasons we might experience pain: God's discipline for disobedience, consequences of our own poor decisions, and fallout from the devil's deception.

God's Discipline for Disobedience

The Bible says, "Know then in your heart that as a man disciplines his son, so the LORD your God disciplines you" (Deuteronomy 8:5). God disciplined Miriam for gossiping about her brother Moses by inflicting her with leprosy (Numbers 12). He disciplined Moses for striking a rock rather than speaking to it as instructed by not allowing him to enter the promised land (Numbers 20:10–13). He disciplined David with three days of pestilence for depending on his army rather than on God's power (2 Samuel 24). Every time we read about God disciplining someone in the Bible, that person knew that the pain they were experiencing was God's discipline for disobedience.

If what we're suffering is God's discipline, we probably won't have to wonder why it's happening or why God allowed it. If it's not clear, then it's probably not discipline—even though the devil will want us to always blame God for every bad thing that happens in our life.

Consequences of Our Own Poor Decisions

Sometimes bad things happen because of our own poor decisions. A decision to have an affair leads to shattered lives. A decision to betray a confidence leads to a broken relationship. A decision to be chronically late for work leads to getting fired. If you jump off of a tall building, you're going to get hurt, or worse. Period. That's not God's doing; it's just the result of a bad decision. Author and psychologist Henry Cloud once said that we are ridiculously in charge of our choices. We can choose to make poor decisions, but we can't choose the consequences of those decisions.

Fallout from the Devil's Deception

Bad things also happen when we succumb to the devil's deception. He's called the "father of lies" (John 8:44 NLT), "the accuser" (Revelation 12:10), and "the thief" (John 10:10); and in Genesis 3:13 he is a deceiver. Jesus tells us, "The thief comes only to steal and kill and destroy" (John 10:10).

We've all seen evil. We know what it looks like and what it feels like, but do we believe that the source of evil is an evil being? When a Barna poll asked American Christians what they believed about the devil, 40 percent "strongly agreed" that Satan "is not a living being but a symbol of evil," and another 19 percent said they "agreed somewhat" with that perspective. Only 35 percent said they believed Satan to be real, and 8 percent weren't sure what they believed about the existence of Satan.[3] If we don't believe in the devil's existence, he's already got a foothold in the fight.

The apostle Paul wrote: "For our struggle is not against flesh and blood, but against the rulers, against the authorities, against the powers of this dark world and against the spiritual forces of evil in the heavenly realms" (Ephesians 6:12).

Yes, there is an active invisible realm of evil that we cannot see. There is also an active invisible realm of warring angels working on our behalf (2 Kings 6:11–17). And while Satan's ultimate battle is against God himself, his schemes play out within the human story. To understand the big picture of why bad things happen, we need to go all the way back to where it first went wrong: the garden, where Satan plays a leading role.

WHERE BROKEN BEGAN

When God fashioned, fitted, and filled the earth, there was nothing but goodness. The lion and the lamb lay side-by-side. Adam and Eve lived a harmonious existence without a hint of discord. God and human beings communed with no barrier between them. All creation ebbed and flowed with the rhythm of the tides and the breath of God. There was no lack, only abundance; no fear, only calm assurance; no violence, only peace; no hatred, only love; no sickness, only health. "God saw all that he had made, and it was very good" (Genesis 1:31). In fact, the Hebrew word that is used for "*very* good" is better translated "*exceedingly* good."[4]

God gave Adam and Eve just one restriction within a bounty of freedom—a restriction that was for their protection and provision. But he also gave them free will: the choice to obey or disobey—to stay within the protective boundaries of his perfect plan or step beyond them.

Adam and Eve had unveiled communion with God, unadulterated community with each other, and unlimited access to all that God had made . . . except for one little thing.

The Tree.

As Lysa TerKeurst pointed out in her book *It's Not Supposed to Be This Way*, it's interesting to note the first three words in God's command to Adam about not eating from the Tree of the Knowledge of Good and Evil: *You are free.* "You are free," he told Adam, "to eat from any tree in the garden; but you must not eat from the tree of the knowledge of good and evil, for when you eat from it you will certainly die."[5] God always speaks the language of freedom. His commands are for our provision and protection because he wants us to live in freedom.

But we know what happened next. Genesis 3 begins with the daunting words, "Now the serpent . . ." The devil slithered into the garden and tempted the pair with the one thing they didn't have. Isn't that just like him? Whatever we don't have, the devil will tell us, "You'd be happy if . . ." He wants us to believe that God is holding out on us:

"You'd be happy if you were married."

"You'd be happy if you were married to someone else."

"You'd be happy if you had children."

"You be happy if those kids were gone."

"You'd be happy if you had a bigger house, more money, a thinner body."

Unfortunately, the "you'd be happy if" lie has introduced a destructive detour into many stories.

The devil launched his plan of deception in the garden by asking a question. "Did God really say, 'You must *not* eat from any tree in the garden'?" (Genesis 3:1, emphasis added). Did you catch that? I loved this nuance when Lysa pointed it out in her book. What God had said was, "You are free . . ." The serpent twisted God's words and said, "Did God really say you must not . . . ?" The devil speaks the language of restriction, twisting God's words to stir up feelings of dissatisfaction.

Anytime we have a thought that essentially begins, "Did God really say," we need to stop and ask, *Where did that thought come from?* Many self-destructive decisions have begun with the question, "Did God really say?" *Did God really say I shouldn't watch that movie? Did God really say I shouldn't reconnect with my old high school boyfriend on Facebook? Did God really say I shouldn't spend money on . . . ?*

In the garden, boundaries God had established to protect Adam and Eve were used by Satan to provoke them instead. He turned God's loving protection into destructive manipulation. Twisting it. Turning it. Bending it. Redefining God's protection as restriction.

Eve's first mistake was engaging the serpent in conversation at all. "We may eat fruit from the trees in the garden," she said, "but God did say, 'You must not eat fruit from the tree that is in the middle of the garden, and you must not touch it, or you will die'" (vv. 2–3).

Eve got it mostly right. God never mentioned not *touching* the fruit, even though that would have been a pretty good idea. However, we should never add what we consider common sense to God's truth. It is true enough standing on its own.

Satan's next words are the first lie recorded in the Bible: "You will not certainly die" (v. 4). In other words, *God is not telling the truth. Sin has no consequences.*

Satan went on to say, "For God knows that when you eat from it your eyes will be opened, and you will be like God, knowing good and evil" (v. 5). In other words, *You can be your own god.*

Eve bought what the devil was peddling and made a disastrous decision that led to the downfall of all creation.

> When the woman saw that the fruit of the tree was good for food
> and pleasing to the eye, and also desirable for gaining wisdom, she
> took some and ate it. She also gave some to her husband, who was

with her, and he ate it. Then the eyes of both of them were opened, and they realized they were naked; so they sewed fig leaves together and made coverings for themselves. (vv. 6–7)

As soon as Adam and Eve sunk their teeth into the forbidden fruit, shame entered the world. The man and woman who were previously naked and felt no shame became the man and woman who cowered and were consumed by shame. Shame blanketed the earth and creation was never the same.

THE FALLOUT OF THE FALL

There were universal consequences of that first cataclysmic decision to disobey God. The Bible says that since that time, the whole earth has been in bondage to death and decay (Romans 8:19–22).

We certainly see that, don't we? Cancer, COVID-19, disease, violence, plane crashes, broken relationships, child abuse, natural disasters—these were not part of God's original good design. And while there are still good things in the world, and while God is still good, creation's good has been tainted with the stain of imperfection, corruption, and decay that God never intended "in the beginning."

Here is how author Philip Yancey described the consequences of what happened in the garden of Eden:

> By their choice they put distance between themselves and God. Before, they had walked and talked with God. Now when they heard his approach, they hid in the shrubbery. An awkward separation had crept in to spoil their intimacy. And every quiver of disappointment in our own relationship with God is an aftershock from their initial act of rebellion.[6]

The original sin of Adam and Eve is often referred to as "the fall." And while it might seem unfair that we have to pay the consequences for someone else's sin, the truth is that we all "fall" every day. The Bible tells us, "For all have sinned and *fall short* of the glory of God'" (Romans 3:23, emphasis added). Just as Adam blamed Eve and Eve blamed the serpent, we tend to look for someone to blame for our difficulties, disappointments, and distresses. Many are quick to blame God when bad things happen, but many bad things happen simply because our world is broken. And our individual stories play out against the backdrop of that brokenness.

It is so important for us to grasp the importance of the fall and its consequences. Without the backdrop of Genesis 3, the question of why bad things happen has no context, which means it will haunt us and halt us at every turn. But when we understand that the whole earth groans as it awaits its liberation from bondage and decay, we know that there is a bigger story to be told.

IT'S NOT ALWAYS GOING TO BE THIS WAY

Here's the good news—I bet you're ready for some good news. Before everything fell apart, God had a plan to put it back together. He didn't leave us in our hopeless state. Jesus, God's Son, put on flesh and stepped into the human story so he could pay the price for our sins, conquer death, and restore our union and communion with God.

One day, the consequences of the fall will be reversed. Jesus will come again, and we will live in the New Jerusalem for all eternity. There will be no more tears, no more death, no more mourning, no more pain. He will make everything new.

I love how author C. S. Lewis described both our current condition and our hope for God's new world:

At present we are on the outside of the world, the wrong side of the door. We discern the freshness and purity of morning, but they do not make us fresh and pure. We cannot mingle with the splendors we see. But all the leaves of the New Testament are rustling with the rumor that it will not always be so. Someday, God willing, we shall get in.[7]

I can't even imagine no more strife, no more disappointment, no more anger. I can't imagine *not* waiting for the other shoe to drop as I make my way on the rocky paths of this life. But I know that day will come. Until then, all of us live in what theologians refer to as "the already but not yet." We live in the in-between space—between when all that was right went wrong, and when all that is wrong will be made right again.

Being followers of Christ does not give us immunity from the effects of living in a fallen world, but it does give us a future and a hope. While our present pain is very real, it is also very temporary— the blink of an eye in the face of eternity. Until Jesus returns, pain will persist, hurts will happen, and tragedy will tear holes in the canvas of our lives. But Ann Voskamp is right—every tear, every rent in the canvas, can become a window through which we see the hand of God.

THE SEE-THROUGH PLACE

Months after losing our baby, God gave me a sweet gift. I was lying in bed trying to picture her in heaven. I wondered what she looked like. I wondered what she was doing. I wondered if I'd recognize her when I get there. Then I pictured her with Jesus, playing. She wasn't sad at all.

In my mind's eye, God pulled back the curtain separating the physical from the eternal and gave me a glimpse of her. It was a see-through place in the torn canvas of my life.

My season of deep mourning ended that night. I stopped asking, "Why me?" and started asking, "What now?" Like a miner with a pickax, I was ready to look for the veins of gold buried in the dark and rocky soil of my suffering. I was ready to learn whatever God wanted me to learn about myself and about trusting in his unfailing love, even when my life felt like it was falling apart.

Just to be clear, I am not saying that I believe God allowed my baby to die just to teach me a lesson. Absolutely not. Life on this side of heaven is filled with loss and disappointment—the consequence of living in a post-Eden world. Jesus meant it when he said, "In this world you will have trouble" (John 16:33). No, I'm not saying God did it; but I am saying God could use it for my good—if I let him.

> *We live in the in-between space—between when all that was right went wrong, and when all that is wrong will be made right again.*

During those days, I sensed God asking, *Will you trust me?* I didn't understand why my narrative was unfolding as it was, and I didn't like this painful twist in the plot, but I did believe that in the end my story would be a good one. I believed it because God is good, and his ways are good. And I believed it because I knew even then that when God allows hurt to happen, he uses the healing of that hurt to give us a purpose we might never have known without it.

I still have days when I long for the little one I never met. Some days, I look at our family portrait of three and see the shadow of a fourth. I know I'll meet her one day. Meanwhile, I trust in the goodness of God who redeems every ounce of pain for our ultimate good. I hold on to the truth that if God says *no* to my plans, it is because he has a greater *yes* in store for me, even though I might not like it or understand it at the time.

A BACKSTAGE PASS TO SUFFERING

Job was a man who had no idea why bad things were happening to him, but we have a backstage pass to watch and learn as his story of suffering unfolds. He lived somewhere between one thousand and fifteen hundred years before Jesus. The man had it all. Seven sons, three daughters, seven thousand sheep, three thousand camels, five hundred yoke of oxen, five hundred donkeys, and a slew of servants. That's a lot of mouths to feed. The Bible says that Job was the greatest man among all the people of the East.

Not only did Job have great wealth, he was also a godly man who made it a habit to pray for his kids every morning. He was "blameless and upright" (Job 1:8). I can't think of anyone I'd call "blameless," but that's how God himself described Job. One would think that a guy like this would receive only blessings from God, but Job's righteousness didn't prevent him from experiencing pain. In fact, it actually made him a candidate for extreme testing. He had no idea why bad things were happening to him, but the pages of Scripture reveal what was going on behind the scenes. Here's how Job ended up in the worst "why me?" experience of his life:

> One day the angels came to present themselves before the LORD, and Satan also came with them. The LORD said to Satan, "Where have you come from?"
>
> Satan answered the LORD, "From roaming throughout the earth, going back and forth on it."
>
> Then the LORD said to Satan, "Have you considered my servant Job? There is no one on earth like him; he is blameless and upright, a man who fears God and shuns evil."
>
> "Does Job fear God for nothing?" Satan replied. "Have you not put a hedge around him and his household and everything he has? You have blessed the work of his hands, so that his flocks and herds

are spread throughout the land. But now stretch out your hand and strike everything he has, and he will surely curse you to your face."

The LORD said to Satan, "Very well, then, everything he has is in your power, but on the man himself do not lay a finger." (vv. 6–12)

Does that scene bother you a little bit? I'll admit it makes me squirm. But hang on. There's more to the story, so let's keep going.

Satan went out from the Lord's presence and got busy. In one day, Job's enemies killed all but a handful of his servants and stole all eleven thousand head of livestock. Then a strong wind collapsed his son's house and killed all ten of Job's children. What was Job's response? "Job got up and tore his robe and shaved his head" (v. 20). In Job's culture, this was a sign of deep mourning. But then he did something that gives me pause: "he fell to the ground in worship." Wait, what? He worshiped? Yep. From the depths of his grief, Job said:

> "Naked I came from my mother's womb,
>   and naked I will depart.
> The LORD gave and the LORD has taken away;
>   may the name of the LORD be praised." (v. 21)

Does it seem odd that Job worshiped God in the midst of such a loss? Perhaps at first. But a broken heart and raised hands are not mutually exclusive; instead, they are a sweet offering to the Lord— perhaps the sweetest. Job was honest with his pain. He didn't sugarcoat it, ignore it, or numb it. Rather, he walked right through it.

Over the next few days, Job broke out with painful sores all over his body. About the only things Job didn't lose were his bitter wife— who told him to "curse God and die" (Job 2:9)—and a handful of friends he would have been better off without. Yet, Job continued to trust God: "Though he slay me, yet will I hope in him" (13:15).

However, when Job was at his lowest point, he couldn't help but cry out in anguish. He blamed God for destroying his honor, his health, and his home—for stripping him of his family, his friends, and his fortune. All the while, God remained mysteriously silent. And while Job *felt* that God had forgotten him, he *knew* that God hadn't. What Job *felt* and what Job *knew* collided.

I've been there. I wonder if you have too.

I *felt* that God deserted me, but I *knew* he would never leave or forsake me.

I *felt* that God didn't care about what was going on in my life, but I *knew* that even one hair on my head didn't fall to the ground without his knowing it.

I *felt* that God wasn't listening, but I *knew* that he was attentive to my prayers.

I *felt* that God wasn't working to remedy my situation, but I *knew* he was always working to bring about my greater good.

Job *felt* that God had deserted him, but he *knew* God hadn't.

Finally, Job reminded his feelings of the facts: "I know that my redeemer lives, and that in the end he will stand on the earth" (19:25). The word translated "redeemer" is the Hebrew word *go'el*. In context it means "kinsman redeemer." In the Old Testament, a kinsman redeemer is a male relative who takes responsibility to act on behalf of a relative who is in trouble, danger, or need. He is one who rescues or redeems a relative from a minor or major emergency. Job knew that God would rescue him; he just didn't know when or how.

Toward the end of Job's story, God broke his silence by posing a few questions of his own to Job:

> Where were you when I laid the earth's foundation?
> Tell me, if you understand.
> Who marked off its dimensions? Surely you know!
> Who stretched a measuring line across it? . . .
> Have you ever given orders to the morning,

or shown the dawn its place,
that it might take the earth by the edges
and shake the wicked out of it? (38:4–5, 12–13)

And that's just a small sampling. The list of God's questions for Job goes on for more than seventy verses across three chapters (38–40). When God finally takes a breath and asks Job to answer, the only thing Job can say is, "I am unworthy—how can I repay you? I put my hand over my mouth" (40:4).

Whenever I read those words, I can't help but bow my head with Job and take a deep breath of my own. *You're right, God. I don't know nothin' 'bout nothin'. You are God and I am not. You don't owe me a thing. I owe you everything. I put my hand over my mouth. As a matter of fact, I put two!*

In another time and place, God would speak these words to the prophet Isaiah: "'For my thoughts are not your thoughts, neither are your ways my ways,' declares the LORD. 'As the heavens are higher than the earth, so are my ways higher than your ways and my thoughts than your thoughts'" (Isaiah 55:8–9).

A human being trying to analyze the mind of God is like a flea trying to analyze the mind of a human being. It's just not possible. But here are two truths we *can* be sure of even when we don't understand God's ways:

"All the ways of the LORD are loving and faithful" (Psalm 25:10).

"Now we see only a reflection as in a mirror; then we shall see face to face. Now I know in part; then I shall know fully, even as I am fully known" (1 Corinthians 13:12).

Here's what hits me every time I get to the end of Job's story: he never knew the *why* of it all. He never got the answers he was looking for. And most likely, on this side of heaven, we won't either. Until then, we place our trust in what we know about who God is—loving and faithful.

THE OTHER SIDE OF WHY

We read the story of Job already knowing how it is going to end—the Lord not only restores what Job had lost, but "gave him twice as much as he had before" (Job 42:10). But can you imagine what it was like to live through it in real time? Job was stuck in a bad story and he saw no end in sight. He had no idea why it was happening. He didn't know God would give him twice as much as he had before. All he knew was loss, disappointment, and pain. That might be where you are right now, stuck in a story you don't like. But hang on, God's pen has not slipped. He's still in control. There's more to come.

My favorite line in Job's story comes at the very end. Job said to God, "My ears had heard of you but now my eyes have seen you" (v. 5). That is my prayer in every difficult circumstance of life. I don't want to simply hear about God; I want to see God and have communion with him in the midst of it. Sometimes the only way to open the unseeing eye and hearken the unhearing ear is through struggle.

A houseful of children was not how my chapter of infertility and the loss of a child ended, but I can still say it had a good ending. One day, I was reading Song of Songs in the Bible. I read it as if I were the bride and Jesus were my bridegroom. At one point, the bride says to her beloved, "I am a rose of Sharon" (2:1).

What did she call herself? God seemed to ask me.

"A rose of Sharon," I whispered. "My name."

Prompted by the Holy Spirit, I looked up the rose of Sharon in my Bible dictionary. I was surprised to learn that Sharon was a fertile valley near Mount Carmel. As I continued to read, God showed me that even though my medical chart had "infertile" stamped across its pages, he had chosen a name for me that meant "fertile valley" long before I was even born.

No, I don't have a houseful of children. God didn't fill the empty rooms of my house as he did Job's. But God has given me spiritual children all around the world. Through ministry and simply obeying God's nudges, I have experienced the joy of birthing spiritual children and nurturing them to maturity. "He gives the barren woman a home," declared the psalmist, "making her the joyous mother of children" (Psalm 113:9 ESV). And, oh, how I love my kids! And when women come to me trying to make sense of the disappointments in their lives, I can say, "Come, sit with me. Let me tell you a story."

Someone once asked me, "Which would you rather have—a house full of biological children or a heart full of spiritual children?"

"I would rather have what God wants me to have," I replied. "Because I know that God's plans for me are much greater than anything I could ever come up with on my own."

Is God still good when his answer is "no"? Yes, he is. Sometimes we have to let go of our plans to take hold of God's purpose.

CRYING IN THE CORNER

Steven was three years old when he contracted a severe case of the flu. His slumped body snuggled listlessly in my lap like a worn-out rag doll. When I carried him into the medical clinic, the doctor took one look at my boy and sent us straight to the hospital. Steven was dehydrated and needed fluids immediately.

My heart ripped wide when the nurses taped a support board to Steven's little arm and inserted the needle for the IV. *Not his thumb-sucking arm*, my heart winced.

"Mommy, Mommy," Steven cried. "Make them stop! They are hurting me!"

"No, honey," I tried to assure him with tears streaming down my cheeks. "They're making you all better."

"Mommy, help me!"

Steven cried. I cried. The nurses cried.

I could only imagine what was going through Steven's mind. *Why are these people hurting me? Why doesn't Mommy make them stop? She must not love me. She's not protecting me. If she loved me, she wouldn't let them do this.*

Standing in the corner watching my little towheaded boy cry, I wondered if God feels something similar when I am in a painful situation. I cry out, "God, help me! Make this stop! Why are you letting this happen? Why are you allowing this person to hurt me? Don't you love me? Don't you care about me? I know you could get me out of this situation if you wanted to. Why don't you make it go away?"

Then I envisioned God speaking to my pain-filled little-girl heart. *You might think I've deserted you, but I will never leave or forsake you. You might think I don't love you, but I love you to the height of heaven and the depth of the sea. You might think I don't care about what's happening to you, but I am orchestrating your days and care about every hair on your head. My ways are higher than your ways and my thoughts are higher than your thoughts. Yes, I do care about you and what is happening to you. In the end, this will make you better. I am not doing something to you; I'm doing something in you.*

Pastor Steven Furtick once said, "We worship a God who can best be explained as a mystery, and yet we live in a culture that worships certainty."[8] However, the very definition of faith is an intertwining of mystery and certainty. The writer of Hebrews penned, "Faith is the assurance of things hoped for, the conviction of things not seen" (Hebrews 11:1 ESV). The word translated "conviction" is the Greek word *elegchos*, which means a proof or test. It can also be translated as "evidence," and yet, faith is belief in something we cannot prove.

There's nothing wrong with trying to understand why bad things happen, but we have to recognize that our understanding is limited. The Bible clearly states, "Trust in the LORD with all your heart and lean not on your own understanding" (Proverbs 3:5). In other words, don't try to figure out everything on your own. When we hold loosely our need to know the *why*, we can trust fully in the *who*. Since God's ways are higher than our ways, we shouldn't expect him to write our stories the same way we would. Often, the twists and turns of the plot won't make sense until we're on the other side of this life. And here's a promise from the Lord himself: "Those who hope in me will not be disappointed" (Isaiah 49:23).

The devil will try to fill in the gaps of what you don't understand and poke holes in what you do. Refuse his input into your situation. Let faith fill the gaps of what you don't understand and the full assurance of God's goodness seal up what you do.

I don't understand why certain parts of my story have played out as they have, and I'm guessing you probably don't either. But one day we will. In the meanwhile, I trust that God loves me and knows what's best for me. That doesn't mean I'm going to like every situation that comes my way, but after I fuss about it for a while, I will settle down and remember that God is not absent in what is happening. I can choose to believe that God will somehow use my pain for a purpose.

Chapter Three

There's Always a Meanwhile

*You don't understand now what I am
doing, but someday you will.*

—Jesus (John 13:7 NLT)

*What?! Dr. Atkinson changed his mind? What do you mean, he changed
his mind? We prayed and felt certain this is what God wanted us to do!
How could we have been so wrong?* Questions and accusations pinged
around my mind as our future fell apart in a matter of moments. But
let me back up and tell the story from the beginning.

While I was in college, I attended a Bible study at a friend's apartment. One night when I walked in, I saw a rugged-looking guy sitting
on the floor. The sleeves of his red flannel shirt were rolled up over
muscular forearms, his chocolate brown eyes made me melt into a
puddle, and his easy laugh was magical. Think Christian Marlboro
man, if you're old enough to remember the billboards. He had a worn
Bible in his lap, Jesus in his heart, and me wrapped around his little
finger. Three and a half months later, we were engaged. Six months
after that, I became his wife.

Steve was in his fourth year of dental school when we married, and

I had just a few more credit hours left to finish up my degree in dental hygiene. His senior year was the time to decide where he wanted to set up his practice. Dentists don't typically move once they get established, so this was a big decision. We prayed. We fasted. We toured various towns and met with several doctors. After several months, we felt certain God was calling us to a little town called Pineville, just outside of Charlotte, North Carolina.

Dr. Atkinson, an older dentist, was looking for a young partner, and everything seemed to fall into place. After graduation, we moved to Charlotte and set up house in a tiny apartment near the office. The rent was half-price for the first three months, which was a huge bonus for a young couple with nothing but school debt on their balance sheet. Smiles all around.

However, when Steve went to the office to finalize his work schedule and management particulars, Dr. Atkinson opened a trapdoor beneath Steve's feet.

"Steve, I've been thinking about it," Dr. Atkinson began, "and I don't think this is such a good idea after all. I've changed my mind."

He extended his hand to my twenty-five-year-old stunned husband and said, "Good luck to you, son."

When Steve came home and told me the news, we were both shell-shocked. "What do you mean, he changed his mind?" I cried. "He can't do that! We've just moved here. He made a commitment!" A host of raw emotions collided with real questions for God. *How could we have been so wrong? Didn't we hear you correctly? We prayed. We fasted. We wanted nothing more than to do what you wanted us to do and go where you wanted us to do it. Now, here we sit in a new city, with a big student loan, no job, no future. What are we supposed to do?* I did not like this story!

I felt like God had left us high and dry. But he hadn't. He was simply moving the puzzle pieces into place for his perfect plan.

Our limited vision doesn't allow us to see *how* God is working behind the questionable scenes in our lives, but we must believe that he is. That's where trust comes in once again. The eighteenth-century spiritual writer Jean-Pierre de Caussade said it well:

> You would be very ashamed if you knew what the experiences you call setbacks, upheavals, pointless disturbances, and tedious annoyances really are. You would realize that your complaints about them are nothing more nor less than blasphemies—though that never occurs to you. Nothing happens to you except by the will of God, and yet [God's] beloved children curse it because they do not know it for what it is.[1]

The truth is, God is always working, whether we recognize it or not. In fact, it may be precisely in the moments we sense him or understand him the least that he is working the most.

Could I believe that? Would I believe that? Steve and I spent days trying to figure out how to respond to this situation. We felt all the stages of grief: denial, anger, bargaining, sadness, and acceptance. Finally, even though we didn't understand the twists and turns of the plot, we dared to trust that God had a better plan—a better story.

SETBACKS OR SETUPS?

Sometimes, it is only after the fact that we understand that what we call setbacks were really God's setups all along. During the days that followed Dr. Atkinson's changing his mind, I worked in two dental offices to get us through. Steve joked that I worked six days a week and cried on the seventh. Then, three months later, a position opened up that had not been available when Steve was first looking. If we had written out our best-case scenario, this situation would have exceeded it by far. We felt like we were living out the promise of Ephesians 3:20

in lab-coat-white: "[God] is able to do immeasurably more than all we ask or imagine, according to his power that is at work within us."

And remember that rent that was half-price for the first three months? It was three months to the day when Steve started in his new position. Who knew? God did. He was not surprised or caught off guard when the first situation fell through. He didn't say, "I didn't see that coming." God was working behind the scenes all along. Our best-case scenario wasn't available until three months after we moved to town. God just needed to get us here first. We experienced God's provision and protection through the twists and turns of uncertainty.

After a few years, the part of town in which Steve had originally planned to practice became a run-down thoroughfare and Dr. Atkinson's office closed down. However, Steve's practice continued to grow. Sometimes God doesn't meet our expectations because he wants to exceed them.

God's sovereignty is best seen on the backdrop of life's uncertainties. What we see as a dead end could be God's door opening to a new beginning. What we feel is a disappointment is often God's divine appointment. What we have in mind is sometimes not what God has in store—and I shout *Thank you, God!* for that. I am so grateful for the right turns in my story when I wanted to turn left. I might not have understood the plot twists at the time, but I praised God for them after the fact.

We live life forward, but we understand it backward. Our limited vision doesn't allow us to see God's strategic maneuvering, but we must believe that he is working still. And even though it may appear that everything is falling apart, it could be that the pieces are actually falling into place. Jesus told his disciples, "You don't understand now what I am doing, but someday you will" (John 13:7 NLT).

I don't know what you're going through right now, but rest assured, God is working for your greater good. When we give up our need to know all the details, we can have a holy confidence that is independent of our circumstances.

TRUSTING WHAT WE CANNOT SEE

Back in the 1960s, cowboy shows on television were the mainstay of every American boy's home. Little guys wore cowboy boots, ten-gallon hats, and six-shooters filled with caps. Some wore five-point sheriff badges; others preferred the bad guy's bandanas covering their lower faces. One repeated phrase in programs such as *The Lone Ranger* or *Rawhide* was, "Meanwhile, back at the ranch." This was a segue from one scene to another that let the viewers know there was more going on than they could see.

> *We live life forward, but we understand it backward.*

In both television shows and real life, "meanwhile" means that while one thing is happening in one place, something else is happening in another. Then, at just the right time, the two things come together for an ah-ha moment that takes our breath away.

Jesus said, "My Father is always at his work to this very day, and I too am working" (John 5:17). Just because we can't see God working, doesn't mean he isn't. He is constantly working on our behalf to bring about his greatest good in our lives.

One of the most poignant examples of God working behind the scenes is the story of Joseph. He was the favorite son of his father, Jacob, born to his father's favorite wife, Rachel (which is another story in itself). However, he was also the least favored sibling of his ten older brothers. You might remember him as the boy with the coat of many colors. His dad made him a fancy jacket that might as well have had the word *favorite* embroidered across the back. And the boy wore it all the time, which was salt in the wound of his less-favorited brothers. I mean, come on, Joe. He was a spoiled kid who tattled on his brothers and puttered about at home, while his older siblings labored in the fields.

Joseph had two dreams about how his brothers and parents would one day bow down to honor him. While he probably should have kept those dreams to himself, immaturity loosened his lips, and he blabbed to his family. The dreams were the sheaves that broke the camel's back, and his brothers despised him even more.

They hated Joseph's coat.

They hated Joseph's dreams.

They hated Joseph, period.

One day, when Joseph was seventeen, his father sent him out to check on his brothers, who were grazing their flocks in the fields. When they saw him coming, his brothers devised a plot to kill him by throwing him into a cistern and leaving him to die. But when they saw an Ishmaelite caravan passing by, they decided to sell Joseph for twenty shekels instead. They pulled him out of the cistern, pushed him into slavery, and pocketed the cash. Then they shredded and bloodied his fancy coat and told their father that his favorite son had been killed by a wild animal. Not far from the truth.

On every step of the two hundred arduous miles to Egypt, Joseph must have been thinking, *This is not how my story is supposed to go.* His dreams had turned into a living nightmare.

I've been there. I bet you have too. Maybe not on a caravan being hauled off to slavery, but on a journey to a destiny that was not what you had imagined. God is constantly writing our stories, and he doesn't give us the next chapters to read in advance. We don't get to see the plot twists and turns until we're smack-dab in the middle of the storyline. Even then, we don't know how all the scenes are going to play out. But we do know that God's pen continues to move even when we feel stuck in a bad place.

Once the caravan reached its destination, we read, "Meanwhile, the Midianites sold Joseph in Egypt to Potiphar, one of Pharaoh's offi-cials, the captain of the guard" (Genesis 37:36, emphasis added). If we were reading this story for the first time, that "meanwhile" might not seem very reassuring. It certainly doesn't sound like God is writing a good story. I'm sure Joseph didn't think so. He was put on a slave trader's auction block and sold to a senior Egyptian official named Potiphar. But "meanwhile" lets us know that something else is going on behind the scenes.

The storywriter goes on to tell us that the Lord was with Joseph and gave him success in everything he did. When Potiphar saw that God's favor was on Joseph, he put him in charge of everything he owned—his entire household. Just when it seemed like there was finally an upswing in the narrative, Joseph faced a dramatic down-swing. But before relating the next scene of the downward spiral, the writer alerts us that "the LORD was with Joseph" (39:2). Hold on to that statement as this next chapter in Joseph's story unfolds. "Now Joseph was well-built and handsome, and after a while his master's wife took notice of Joseph and said, 'Come to bed with me!'" (vv. 6–7).

Potiphar's wife tried her best to get Joseph to do his worst. After several failed attempts, Joseph fled her presence. Unfortunately, she was holding on to his cloak when he hightailed it out of there. She must have had a pretty tight grip. Joseph left with his resolve in place, but his reputation in her hands. She screamed attempted rape, and Potiphar hauled Joseph off to prison for something he didn't do.

Again, from the outside looking in, this does not read like a good story, even though the narrative affirms that "the LORD was with Joseph" just before it happened. From our vantage point three thou-sand years later, we know that God was fitting together all the puzzle pieces to match the box-top picture he had designed long ago. But for Joseph, there were only unanswered questions, unresolved conflicts, and unjust accusations. Off to prison he went for another confusing chapter.

"But while [*meanwhile*] Joseph was there in the prison, the LORD was with him; he showed him kindness and granted him favor in the eyes of the prison warden" (vv. 20–21). There it is again: "The LORD was with him." Did Joseph feel God's favor at the time? Did he tell all his cellmates how good God was to him? I doubt it. Thirteen years is a long time to serve as a slave and prisoner for a crime you didn't commit. But Joseph's story was written long after the fact—and it's usually in the "after the fact" that we see how God's meanwhile was working to make a masterpiece out of our difficult chapters.

In Joseph's meanwhile, God placed two of Pharaoh's ousted servants—the cupbearer and the baker—in prison at the same time. One day, Joseph noticed the pair looking dejected and asked what was wrong.

> "We both had dreams," they answered, "but there is no one to interpret them."
>
> Then Joseph said to them, "Do not interpretations belong to God? Tell me your dreams." (40:8)

It was no coincidence that Pharaoh's cupbearer, his baker, and Joseph were in prison simultaneously. God was working to get them in position to be a part of his plan. Then, at the right time, their lives intersected so Joseph could interpret their dreams. And right now, you can rest assured that God is working in the lives of people you've never met, in places you've perhaps never been, to accomplish his purposes in ways you never could have imagined. Your difficult story may seem like a setback, but it might just be a setup for God's unfolding plan.

Did Joseph like how the first thirty years of his life were being written? I doubt it. I don't think he walked around singing the ancient equivalent of Pharrell Williams's song "Happy." He wanted a new chapter and a very different story. He essentially told the cupbearer, "When you get out of prison, mention me to the Pharaoh and GET ME

OUT OF THIS PLACE! I DIDN'T DO ANYTHING WRONG!"
Sorry for the all caps. That's my personal interpretation. I would not
have said those words quietly or with a smile on my face. I don't think
Joseph did either.

Two years later, Joseph's ex-cellmate, Pharaoh's cupbearer, did
remember him. But don't let that fact slip by you: *two years later.*
That's a long time for the *Jeopardy* theme song to be playing in your
head while waiting for God to do something about your stinky
situation.

When Pharaoh had a dream no one could interpret, the cupbearer
told his boss, "I know a guy." With God's help, Joseph interpreted
Pharaoh's dream, predicting seven years of plenty followed by seven
years of famine. Pharaoh was so impressed, he made Joseph second
in command over all of Egypt. In one day, Joseph went from being a
ragged prisoner to a royal prince of Egypt (42:6).

Eleven years later, when Joseph's brothers came searching for food
during the famine, they were terrified to find their sibling in charge.
I'm sure they were even more surprised with their brother's wise words
of grace: "I am your brother Joseph, the one you sold into Egypt! And
now, do not be distressed and do not be angry with yourselves for
selling me here, because it was to save lives that *God sent me* ahead of
you" (45:4–5, emphasis added).

Did you catch that? "You *sold* me," Joseph told his brothers, "but
God *sent* me."

Later, Joseph would say to these same brothers, "You intended to
harm me, but God intended it for good to accomplish what is now
being done, the saving of many lives" (50:20). Joseph was in a position
of power. He could easily have exacted revenge and made his brothers
pay for what they had done to him. Instead, he chose to embrace God's
sovereign plan and spared them.

Yes, Joseph eventually saw his *why.* He framed his suffering
within the sovereignty of God and discovered a greater purpose that

redeemed his pain. Joseph developed a divine perspective on his story because he understood how it showcased the bigger story God was writing.

Even if we never see our *why* as Joseph did, we might still be able to look back and see the signs of God's *meanwhile* at work—if we look closely enough. Sometimes the sequence of events in our lives seems as randomly placed as body parts in a Picasso painting or as convoluted as a crayon-drawn map by a two-year-old's chubby hand. But even if the sequence of events in our lives doesn't make sense, we can trust in the God who knows the beginning from the end, who's already scripted the closing scene before it even begins. His sovereign pen does not slip or falter.

Think of a caterpillar in a cocoon. Think of a baby in the womb. Think of a seed in the ground. All of these are reminders of the hidden ways God is always at work. When we go through difficult times, it is easy to think God is aloof. We ask, "Why me?" and feel pretty sure we're not going to get an answer. But even though we might not get the answer we're looking for, we can be sure of this—God is *always* working behind the scenes. There is always a *meanwhile* that will make our pain *worthwhile*.

DISAPPOINTMENTS ON THE ROAD TO DESTINY

I had one of my first experiences of God's meanwhile ways when I was a senior in high school. At the time, all my friends were making plans for college, and I was hoping to go along with them. However, as my parents had not gone to college themselves, neither I nor they had any idea where to start. But I was determined to have a different story than the one I had growing up, so I was resolute about going to college. When a classmate mentioned that she was going to the University of

North Carolina at Chapel Hill to major in dental hygiene, I wasn't sure what a hygienist was, but I liked the sound of it. So, I decided I would do that too. Boom. Decision made.

By the time I applied to the program, it was full. A rejection letter invited me to try again the following year. I didn't like that idea. So, I moved to another town and enrolled in a two-year program at a community college. Two years later, I had an associate's degree in dental hygiene, a license to practice, and a job in my hometown. The only problem was that all my friends were still away at school. I was miserable and lonely. When we got together on weekends, their conversations and experiences were very different from the ones I had during my 8:00–5:00 workday with a one-hour lunch break.

Just as they were finally graduating from college, I decided to go back to college. I'd saved up money and sent in another application to the program at Chapel Hill. This time, I was accepted. Four years after I originally planned to start at this school, I began my freshman classes for a bachelor's degree.

It just so happened (I hope you don't believe that for a moment) that was the same year Steve Jaynes started his junior year at the same school. Six weeks after I got to school, I walked into that Bible study I mentioned earlier and met my destiny. If I had not been rejected the first time I applied, I would have missed one of the greatest blessings of my life. God was working in my meanwhile, and what I initially saw as a setback was God's setup to get the characters of my story in the right place at the right time.

As John Piper once said, "In every situation you face, God is always doing a thousand different things that you cannot see, and you do not know."[2] That might be where you are today, right now. Perhaps you're hanging on by a thread, trying to keep your story from unravelling. Perhaps you're holding your breath, waiting for the next shoe to drop. You may feel like God isn't working on your behalf or that your prayers are simply bouncing around the cosmos. Don't be fooled by what you see with your eyes. God is always working in ways you may never know.

All the struggles that happen in our meanwhiles have the potential to develop us. God is preparing us for what he has prepared for us. That is as true for you and me as it was for Moses, who took care of sheep for forty years to learn how to shepherd people, or David, who was forced to run from King Saul and in the process learned how to run a nation. It's as true for you and me as it was for Martha, who watched her brother die so she could tell others about the Messiah who raised him from the dead. What we see as trouble, God sees as training. We can't take an escalator to holiness. We have to ascend the stairway of struggle to strengthen our legs and pace our steps.

IT RARELY "IS WHAT IT IS"

I often hear people say, "It is what it is." What they mean is, *The situation is not going to change, so just accept it.* Let me tell you why I don't like that saying. "It" rarely is what it looks like it is. In fact, what we think the situation is, usually isn't what it is at all.

The Old Testament story of Ruth and Naomi is a perfect example of something not being at all what it looks like it is. I like to think of the four little chapters that tell this story as God weaving a tapestry in which we see only the backside—tangled knots and crisscrossing threads—until the very end. Not until the last page, when God flips the tapestry over, do we get to see how he had been weaving the frayed strands of Ruth and Naomi's struggle during the meanwhile of their story.

Naomi was a young girl when she met and married Elimelech. His name meant "God is King," and she knew that he would always serve the living God of Israel. Like most young Hebrew women, I'm sure she had dreamed of living her days in Bethlehem with strapping young sons, beautiful daughters-in-law, and a passel of grandchildren crowding around her feet. But that was not her story.

Naomi did have two sons, but they weren't what she'd hoped for. One boy she named Mahlon, which means "puny or weakling," and the other she named Kilion, which means "pining." Oh well.

While the boys were still young, a famine hit Bethlehem. Elimelech made a short-sighted decision to move his family to Moab "for a while," just long enough for the famine to pass (Ruth 1:1). Unfortunately, his "for a while" turned into "a long while." However, God was working in the meanwhile to provide for Naomi in a way she could have never imagined.

Moab was a grain-filled plateau east of the Dead Sea. It wasn't a land suitable for farming, but the inhabitants could raise goats and sheep on the plentiful grains. The Moabites worshiped foreign gods, and the Lord forbade intermarriage. However, when Mahlon and Kilion came of age, they married Moabite women anyway.

Over a ten-year period, Naomi's life took a turn for the worse. When her husband and both sons died, Naomi and her two daughters-in-law, Orpah and Ruth, had no male in the family to take care of them, as was the custom. Worse still, Naomi had no one to carry on the family name and no chance of grandchildren—her future was barren. This was not a story any woman in her situation would like.

But Naomi had heard that the famine in Bethlehem was over. So she encouraged both of her daughters-in-law to return to their mothers' homes and find Moabite men to marry, while she planned to return to her homeland. Orpah agreed to stay behind, but Ruth refused. She pled to stay with Naomi.

> "Don't urge me to leave you or to turn back from you. Where you
> go I will go, and where you stay I will stay. Your people will be my

people and your God my God. Where you die I will die, and there
I will be buried. May the LORD deal with me, be it ever so severely,
if even death separates you and me." (Ruth1:16–17)

Both Naomi and Ruth knew that most Israelites despised
Moabites. They had never forgiven the Moabites for hiring Balaam
to place a curse on them after they left Egypt for the promised land
many years before (Numbers 22–24). Regardless of the opposition she
would face, Ruth still desired to go with Naomi.

Reluctantly, Naomi allowed Ruth to return with her to Bethlehem.
After an arduous journey, the two dusty and exhausted women reached
their destination. When they walked into town, people whispered
among themselves. "Could this be Naomi? It looks like her and yet it
doesn't."

Naomi was so downcast and discouraged that her very counte-
nance made her unrecognizable to those she had known before. She
had gone away married and wealthy only to return widowed and
poor. When Naomi heard the whispers as she walked by, she stopped
and said,

"Don't call me Naomi [which means pleasant]. . . . Call me Mara
[which means bitter], because the Almighty has made my life very
bitter. I went away full, but the LORD has brought me back empty.
Why call me Naomi? The LORD has afflicted me; the Almighty has
brought misfortune upon me." (Ruth 1:20–21)

There's no doubt who Naomi blamed for her misfortune. Even
the name she used for God, *El Shaddai*, which means "the Almighty"
or "All-Sufficient One," is laced with sarcasm. It's as if she was saying,
*You people might call Yahweh the "All-Sufficient One," but he sure hasn't
been all-sufficient to me!*

I've heard the same resentment toward God in the voices of others experiencing disappointment and discouragement. I bet you have too. For some of us, the voice we heard was our own. It may feel that God is on a long lunch break during our difficult chapters, but remember, there's always a meanwhile. Oh, how I want to get that! Oh, how I want you to get that too. He *is* the Almighty, the All-Sufficient One, whether or not we can feel it in the moment.

Naomi didn't blame her husband for making a poor decision; she didn't blame the famine for making her hungry; she didn't blame her Moabite friends for not pitching in to help. She blamed God. In a sense, she was correct. God is sovereign and in control of every aspect of our lives. However, he was not out to get her. His hand was not against her. He wasn't intent on afflicting her, as she claimed. Naomi was so blinded by grief and bitterness she couldn't recognize God's gracious provision walking right beside her in the form of a Moabite girl whose name meant "woman friend."

Fortunately for Naomi, Ruth was no slouch. Once they arrived, she decided to go out and glean wheat behind the pickers—to gather the scraps others dropped while working. Even though she knew it would be dangerous for a Moabite woman to venture into an Israelite field, she took a chance in order to provide for herself and Naomi.

Okay, now, picture this. There must have been dozens of fields she could have picked. Pick a field, any field. She picked one, or did she?

"*As it turned out*, she was working in a field belonging to Boaz, who was from the clan of Elimelek" (2:3, emphasis added). Another translation says, "Now she *just happened to* end up in the portion of the field belonging to Boaz, who was from the clan of Elimelech" (v. 3 NET, emphasis added).

She just happened to end up in Boaz's field? I hope you don't believe that for a minute. I can almost see God pointing her in the right direction. Boaz was Ruth's deceased husband's kinfolk, a relative Naomi had all but forgotten—though God hadn't forgotten at all. He was working in the meanwhile faster than those gleaners could bundle those sheaves. I can almost see God's hand under Boaz's chin, lifting his head and pointing his eyes toward the beautiful stranger gleaning among the stalks.

Jon Bloom wrote this in regard to Ruth and Naomi's meanwhile:

This is what we must remember in our times of desolation, grief, and loss. How things appear to us and how they actually are, are rarely the same. Sometimes it looks and feels like the Almighty is dealing "very bitterly" with us when all the while he is doing us and many others more good than we could have imagined.[3]

Boaz noticed Ruth, invited her to eat at his table, and made sure the reapers left more than enough behind for her to glean. In the end, Boaz became Naomi's *go'el,* her kinsman redeemer, when he also became Ruth's husband.

Shortly after Boaz and Ruth were married, she conceived and bore a son named Obed. Obed became the father of Jesse, who became the father of King David, who was in the lineage of Jesus. Maybe that's when Naomi told her friends to stop calling her bitter Mara and go back to calling her pleasant Naomi.

The women said to Naomi: "Praise be to the LORD, who this day has not left you without a guardian-redeemer. May he become famous throughout Israel! He will renew your life and sustain you in your old age. For your daughter-in-law, who loves you and who is better to you than seven sons, has given him birth." (4:14–15)

If we're not careful, we can end up bitterly stuck rather than pleasantly surprised. When we look at life through the difficulties of yesterday rather than the possibilities of today, we just might miss the grains of goodness God leaves behind.

You might wonder why I keep going back to these biblical stories, especially when the difficult situations we face today seem far removed from them. It's because there is so much hope in these stories. The writer of Romans tells us: "For everything that was written in the past was written to teach us, so that through the endurance taught in the Scriptures and the encouragement they provide we might have hope" (Romans 15:4).

Yes, Ruth and Naomi lived several thousand years ago, but they were women just like you and me. They struggled with their husbands, their kids, their friends, their emptiness, and their disappointment with difficult circumstances. All of it. God made sure that these stories were in the Bible to teach us, train us, and give us hope.

My pastor, Chris Payne, often says, "If you want to see what God is saying, look at what he has said. If you want to know what God is doing, look at what he has done." God wove his purposes throughout Ruth and Naomi's *meanwhile*, and at just the right time, he flipped the tapestry to reveal the masterpiece of his weaving. *Voila!* And he will do the same for you and me.

Chapter Four

The Scab You Won't Stop Picking

Yesterday is gone. Tomorrow has not yet
come. We have only today. Let us begin.

—Mother Teresa

Five-year-old Brooke was sitting in the backseat of the minivan while her mom and I ran errands. "Mommy," she asked, "is it worse to pick a scab or pick a mosquito bite?

"You shouldn't pick either one," her mom replied.

I glanced back at Brooke as she tried to wipe away the bloody evidence that she had done both.

Little girls aren't the only ones who pick at scabs. We big girls do it too. Maybe we don't pick at the brown crusty scabs that form over flesh wounds, but we do pick at bitter rusty scabs that form over soul wounds. Either way, picking at scabs keeps wounds from healing and keeps us stuck from moving forward in our stories.

I once met a woman I'll call Meghan, who was a scab picker. She had sad brown eyes, cropped curly hair, and shoulders rounded beyond her years. She sat on the front row in a middle seat at a women's

47

conference where I was teaching. Meghan nodded her head at appropriate times and even voiced an amen or two.

At the break, Meghan waited for me at the foot of the stage steps. We sat side by side and she told me her story. Meghan had been sexually abused as a child and sent to live with an aunt and uncle. This couple mistreated her as well until she left their home. After high school, she married a man who became a pastor. But her childhood abuse had left her with an aversion to sex, and so she preferred to sleep on her own in a separate bedroom. She said her husband had repeatedly forced himself on her and treated her harshly. This was a bad story. My heart broke for her.

I'm not sure if Meghan remembered or not, but she had previously emailed me her story, almost word for word. At the conference, I spoke about how to get unstuck from the cycle of a bad story—some of which you'll read in the following pages.

During the corporate prayer time, many women came forward to pray with members of the conference ministry team. Meghan was one of those at the altar. I was thrilled, hoping for a breakthrough. Later that day, I asked the woman who had prayed with Meghan how it went. I could tell she was frustrated. "She told me her story," she said, "but she didn't seem interested in moving past it or being free of it. She just wanted to talk about it. I prayed for her, but I don't think she was interested in moving beyond where she is right now. She said she wanted to get better, but she just kept repeating the details of what she'd been through."

In all the telling and retelling, Meghan never once stated that she wanted healing from the hurt or freedom from past pain. It seemed as if her story had become who she was and always would be. I imagine it terrified her to think what her life might be without it. Every time she picked at the scab by telling and retelling her trauma, the wound split open and bled once again. Please don't think me harsh. Everyone has their own process and time frame for healing. But at some point, there are also a few questions we have to ask ourselves:

> *Do I really want to stop the cycle of being stuck in a bad story?*
> *Do I really want to get well and move forward?*
> *Do I really want my worst chapters to become my greatest victories,*
> *knowing that it's going to take some work to get there?*

Even though it might seem like the obvious answer is yes, that's not always the case. When it comes to healing, we have to really want it, which is why Jesus posed the question he did to a suffering man.

DO YOU WANT TO GET WELL?

One day, Jesus went up to Jerusalem for a feast. While he was there, he stopped by the pool of Bethesda. The pool was surrounded by five covered colonnades or verandas, which was a gathering place for a great number of suffering people—those who were blind, lame, or otherwise infirm. The people believed that from time to time an angel would come down from heaven and stir the waters. The first one in the water afterward would be healed. So, there they sat, day after day, staring at the water and waiting for the mysterious rippling.

A man, who had been an invalid for thirty-eight years, caught Jesus' eye. When Jesus learned the man had been in this condition for such a long time, he asked him, "Do you want to get well?" (John 5:6).

That is a strange question—or is it?

Sometimes we grow accustomed to being stuck in a bad story. Sure, there are heartaches and heartbreaks, disappointment and disillusionment, fear and fragile emotions, but at least we know what to expect out of life. A wound can become so precious to us that it becomes something we wear as a badge of honor in some strange way. It might make us feel special because it elicits sympathy or deferential treatment. We might cling to a bad story because there is some comfort in it—it fits like a well-worn shoe. However painful the past may have been, it can also feel more stable than the uncharted territory of living without it. Sometimes we prefer to live in the certainty of dysfunction rather than embrace the uncertainty of change. At that point, we can become so attached to our wounds that they become part of who we are.

Pain we're unwilling to let go of can become an idol. Not that we worship it in a god sense, but we essentially worship it as a powerful force that controls our lives—a force over which we mistakenly believe we have no control. We can't imagine life without it. In our minds, the wounded state becomes our normal condition. We mistakenly think, *This is just how my marriage is . . . This is just how my finances are . . . This is just how my emotions roll . . . This is just who I am.* Once we surrender to the this-is-just-who-I-am mindset, we become stuck in the bad parts of our stories, unable to move forward even when healing is available.

> *Sometimes we prefer to live in the certainty of dysfunction rather than embrace the uncertainty of change.*

For the lame man by the pool, healing would require some drastic changes. He would have to get a job and learn some sort of trade, particularly since begging was all he'd ever known. He would have to stand on his own two feet, literally and figuratively. So, he had to wrestle with the implications of Jesus' question: *Do I want to get well? Hmmm. I'm not sure. At least I know what to expect in this condition. Let me think about that.*

The first step to healing from trauma, no matter how it happened, is to decide that we want to get well—that we want a better story. We may not have deserved or caused the wound, but that's what we got. And we will never move forward into a new chapter until we are willing to let go of the old one.

TAKE UP YOUR MAT

So, let's get back to Jesus' question: "Do you want to get well?"

Stranger than Jesus' question to the lame man was the lame man's answer to Jesus. It was a simple yes-or-no question, not a discussion question. But rather than answer Jesus' question, the man gave a justification for his condition: "Sir, . . . I have no one to help me into the pool when the water is stirred. While I am trying to get in, someone else goes down ahead of me" (v. 7).

In other words, *It's not my fault. It's everybody else's fault. This is just how things work around here.* It's fine to explain how we got to be a certain way, as long as we don't use it as an excuse to stay that way. The man clung to his affliction and blamed his condition on those around him—he was a victim of circumstance.

We don't know if he had lost the will to be healed, was afraid to lose the income of a beggar, or simply had accepted lameness as his lot in life. Whatever the case, when he came face-to-face with someone who could set his feet to dancing, he wasn't sure how to respond.

Even though the man never did answer Jesus' question, Jesus stepped over his excuses and said, "Get up! Pick up your mat and walk" (v. 8). And he did.

Jesus had a knack for telling people to do what they didn't think they could.

> *Stretch out the fingers of your withered hand.*
> *Stand up straight and unbend your back.*
> *Roll the stone away and let the dead man out.*
> *Open your blind eyes and tell me what you see.*

Notice Jesus didn't ask the man if he wanted to feel better. He wasn't and isn't satisfied with us simply feeling better in our bad stories. He wants us to be healed from the wounds of the past, no matter how we received them. And he *wants* us to *want* to be healed. If we don't, then we won't.

Many want to be comforted in their dysfunction but not healed from what wounded them or the stuck patterns that keep them there. I suspect that was the case with Meghan, whom I met at the conference. But God doesn't want to simply comfort you in your distress. He wants to heal you from the history of hurt that caused it. He wants to give you the power to do what you never thought you could. He wants to raise you up to places you never thought he would. When the flesh cries, "I would if I could!" the Spirit replies, "You could if you would."

We all have some kind of condition. Maybe it's not as visible as that of the lame man by the pool, but we have something in our stories that holds us back, something we'd like to change. And Jesus asks us the same question: *Do you want to get well?* It's paralyzing to live in the past. Jesus provides the way to move forward—to pick up our mats and walk.

> *God doesn't want to simply comfort you in your distress. He wants to heal you from the history of hurt that caused it.*

Once we say yes, we've taken the first step, but that doesn't mean healing is instantaneous. In fact, healing often takes more time than we think it should. I discovered a great illustration of this when I read that, back in the 1980s, scientists discovered a formula to clean away 370 years of accumulated soot and grime from Michelangelo's masterpiece on the ceiling of the Sistine Chapel. It took four years for Michelangelo to paint his masterpiece, but it took eight years for restorers to clean it. In our own lives, healing from the most difficult parts of our stories may take twice as long as it did for the painful chapter to be written in the first place. And maybe even longer. Even so, healing starts with a determined decision that says:

I will not live bitter.
I will not live angry.
I will not live disappointed.
I will not live discouraged.
I will not live wounded.
I will not live shamed.
I will not live as a victim of circumstances but as a victor who is equipped by God, enveloped in Jesus Christ, and empowered by the Holy Spirit. And it starts now.
Yes, I want to be well.

Whew! I feel better already.

Thirty-eight years is a long time for the lame man by the pool of Bethesda to be immobile, and yet, I was immobile in my bad story for about the same amount of time. No, I wasn't physically paralyzed; I was emotionally paralyzed. Feelings of inferiority, insecurity, and inadequacy held me captive. Harsh words held me hostage; dark memories kept life small. Then Jesus asked me, *Do you want to get well?* After thirty-eight years, I finally said yes. The cross was the bridge I walked across to get out of a stuck story and move on to a new and better chapter.

WHEN CLOCKS STOP TICKING

Back in 1860, Charles Dickens wrote the classic novel *Great Expectations.* No need to break out in a sweat if you're thinking, *I was supposed to read that in high school, but I never did!* You can relax—I didn't read it in high school either. But I did read it recently.

One of the most memorable characters in the novel is an elderly spinster named Miss Havisham. When the main character, a young boy named Pip, is taken to her Gothic estate, he sees a dismal old brick structure with partially boarded-up windows and rusted iron bars. But more startling than the rundown appearance of the outside of the house is what he finds inside.

Miss Havisham, the lady of the manor, sits in a tattered and yellowed wedding gown that hangs over her skeletal frame. Paper-thin skin wraps itself around her claw-like hands. A rotting veil rests upon her gray wispy hair. One shoe sits on a side table, as if waiting to be placed on her foot with the other. Bridal flowers, now long dead, adorn her head. To add to the oddities, Pip notices that every clock in the room has stopped at twenty minutes till nine. In fact, every clock in the house ticked its last at twenty minutes till nine.

Pip later learns that many years before, Miss Havisham had been dressing for her wedding day when she received the heart-rending news that her fiancé had run off with another woman. He would not be marrying her after all. From that moment on, life stopped for Miss Havisham. Every room was left as it was. The wedding cake still lay rotting. The gardens were overrun with weeds. Time stood still for the jilted bride. Miss Havisham patted her heart, looked at Pip, and said, "Broken." She had sacrificed her future on the altar of her past, refusing to let it go.

What a picture!

It's an unfortunate fact that the human brain tends to remember negative events more vividly than positive ones. Different hemispheres of the brain handle these positive and negative emotions, and negative emotions and events require more thinking, processing, and ruminating to absorb.[1] That's why unpleasant events are so deeply engrained in our minds.

Scientists have also shown that, while men tend to remember events, women tend to remember both the events and the emotions attached to them.[2] It's the emotions that keep us picking at scabs—fearing that if we stopped, we might forget or, worse, lose our identity as it relates to the trauma.

The apostle Paul wrote, "Get rid of all bitterness, rage and anger, brawling and slander, along with every form of malice" (Ephesians 4:31). The Greek word translated *bitterness* is *pikria*, which means "bitterness or harshness." As Paul used the word, it conveys an embittered or resentful spirit. The root word *pik* sounds like what it means: pick, prick, or cut. It can refer to a sharp or pointed object or a bitter, sharp taste. Used figuratively, it describes "that angry and resentful state of mind that can develop when we undergo troubles."[3]

When we keep picking at the scab of past pain, refusing to allow the wound to heal, we will become bitter. And bitterness spawns other undesirable emotions and actions. Look at the words Paul tethered to bitterness: *rage, anger, brawling, slander, malice.* A bitter root will produce bitter fruit. It has no choice. This is what happens when we, like Miss Havisham, hold our fingers on the hands of the clock to stop life from moving on and thus invite bitterness to take root. Of course, life forges ahead, clock or no clock. It is only the ticking clock of the heart that stays stuck as the world continues to spin.

WHEN THE MIND KEEPS REVIEWING

Whether it is the mistakes made through us or the mistreatment done to us, those events are etched in our minds forever. And yet, the apostle Paul made it clear that it is possible to put the past in the past. He wrote, "One thing I do: Forgetting what is behind and straining toward what is ahead, I press on toward the goal to win the prize for which God has called me heavenward in Christ Jesus" (Philippians 3:13–14). The key to being able to leave the past behind is in understanding the word *forget.*

A good place to start is with the statements God himself has made about forgetting. God said, "I will forgive their wickedness and will remember their sins no more" (Jeremiah 31:34). But how does an omniscient God who knows all things all the time "forget" anything or "remember them no more"? Let's consider the opposite of forgetting—remembering—to see if the antonym sheds any light. With remembering, we have the same dilemma. How does an omniscient God who already knows all things at all times "remember" something?

There are many events in the Bible that begin with the words "God remembered." Here are just a few:

- "God remembered Noah" (Genesis 8:1).
- "[God] remembered Abraham" (Genesis 19:29).
- "God remembered Rachel" (Genesis 30:22).
- "God heard their groaning and remembered his covenant with Abraham, with Isaac and with Jacob" (Exodus 2:24).

In each incident, God's remembering someone meant he was about to do something—he was about to act on their behalf.

If God *remembering* means he is about to act, then God *forgetting* means that he is *not* going to act. When he forgets our sins, he chooses not to act on them by punishing us. As humans, we tend to remember what we need to forget and forget what we need to remember. God, on the other hand, forgets what he promises to forget and remembers what he promises to remember. He is able to blot out our sins so completely that even the tiniest hint of stain is gone. The psalmist declared, "As far as the east is from the west, so far has he removed our transgressions from us" (Psalm 103:12).

While we cannot forget the wounds of our past, we can choose not to act on them. We can choose to forgive the person who has hurt us and not allow the memory to control our lives. In that sense, we *can* forgive and forget. We'll talk more about forgiveness in the next chapter, so hold that thought.

When Paul talks about "forgetting what is behind," he does not mean that he somehow wiped the past from his memory. Instead, he made a decision described by one scholar as "a conscious refusal to let [the past] absorb his attention and impede his progress."[4] Paul refused to allow anything from his past to control his present. He didn't allow the past to paralyze his potential for the future. Instead, he used the past to fuel his faith as he moved toward what lay ahead.

The truth is, we can never truly forget what has happened in our past. And that's actually a good thing—if we forgot our mistakes and failures, we'd be likely to repeat them. All we can do is mourn the moments we can never get back, learn what we can from them under the tutelage of the Holy Spirit, and then move on.

What did Paul have to forget? He had been unjustly beaten with rods, flogged with whips, pelted with stones, locked in prison, persecuted by fellow Jews, and threatened by Gentiles he was trying to help. He often went without food, without clothes, and without a pillow on which to lay his head (2 Corinthians 11:23–29). That is a lot worse than someone hurting your feelings. And yet, Paul essentially said, "I let it go so I can move on to something better."

Not only did Paul have to forget what was done *to* him by others; he also had to forget what was done *through* him—the atrocities he committed against Christians before he came to Christ. Paul had followers of Christ arrested, beaten, and murdered. That blood is hard to wash from a person's hands. And yet, through the grace of Jesus, he did.

Yes, I remember the wounds from my past, but I can honestly say I no longer act on them. When I remember, I don't feel the resentment, bitterness, or shame of my early years. My past may color my present, but it no longer controls it. Because the memories have so little power over my actions and emotions these days, they come to the surface much less often. This is how I "forget" what is behind and recall how God has redeemed my story at the same time.

Thousands of years ago, the prophet Isaiah used a vivid image that demonstrates how important it is to let go of the past:

> When a farmer plows for planting, does he plow continually?
> Does he keep on breaking up and working the soil?
> When he has leveled the surface,
>   does he not sow caraway and scatter cumin?
> Does he not plant wheat in its place,
>   barley in its plot,
>   and spelt in its field? (Isaiah 28:24–25)

Some of us have been plowing and replowing the soil of our wounds far too long. We've been telling and retelling what was done and how it was done . . . going over the same ground and stirring up the same dirt into a giant dust bowl of pain and regret. But there comes a point when it is time to stop plowing and start planting, to stop picking the scab and allow it to heal. Until then, we will never see a harvest—we will never experience our greatest victories.

WHEN A BAD STORY LEADS TO A GOOD PURPOSE

There are a handful of popular television programs these days on flipping houses. Someone purchases a dilapidated house for pennies on the dollar, spends weeks tearing down the old and building up the new, and then sells the house for a profit. It's fascinating to watch beat-up houses be transformed into beautiful homes. What's even more fascinating is watching God take beat-up lives and transform them into beautiful stories. That's a transformation I was privileged to witness in my friend Anna.

Anna sat with one of her clients on the blue-and-green upholstered chairs of the church counseling office. Barbara's childhood sexual abuse had seeped into her adulthood relationships and she was looking for help. She didn't enjoy sexual intimacy, had trouble trusting friends, and preferred isolation to socialization. After forty-five minutes of spilling her heart out, Barbara lamented, "What's the use? You could never understand!"

"Oh, Barbara," Anna began as she looked deep within the woman's eyes. "Let me tell you a story." And so, it began.

Anna was born into a military family that moved around the country and overseas every one to three years. Over an eighteen-year span, they lived in the Philippines, Colorado, Florida, California, and Tennessee. She, her twin sister, and two older siblings had trouble building relationships because they were constantly being uprooted. Her mom was an alcoholic homemaker, and her dad spent most of his time with his mistress, the United States Air Force.

When Anna was very young, her mom often took the twins to spend time at Grandma and Grandpa's house. Anna's grandpa was a jovial older man who talked to the animals, carried candy in his pocket, and whistled as he walked. But, and here it comes, there was a sinister side to Grandpa that nobody knew about.

Anna's grandparents had a wooden work shed out back on their property. Gray shingles covered the top and three sides. A creaky door on rusted hinges swung out from the fourth. The shed had no windows, but light snuck in through the cracks in the poorly constructed walls. She still remembers the dank smell of the musty dirt floor, the creepy mix-match of old yard tools hanging from nails on the unfinished walls, and the glare from a single bulb dangling from the low-hanging ceiling. Like clockwork, a midday train blared its horn when going down the tracks right behind their house.

"Let's go out to the shed for a bit," he'd call to one or the other of the twin girls. Anna went. She didn't think she could say no. It was in that shed that her grandpa groped her little body, penetrated her private places, and warned her to never tell. "This is our secret," he'd whisper when the deed was done. "If you tell, somebody's going to get hurt, and it might be you."

The sexual abuse went on for five years. Anna felt alone with her secret until one day her twin sister confided that it was happening to her too. Together, they told their mom. "Just stay away from him and it will be okay," she said with a shrug.

The girls couldn't believe it! That was all she had to say? It would be many years before either Anna or her sister trusted anyone again. It would be even more years before they would discover that Grandpa had molested their mother too.

"Barbara," Anna said gently to her client, "I do understand." Anna said she could see the weight begin to fall from Barbara's shoulders as she realized that she was not alone.

How did Anna move from being a scab picker to a hope-giver and healer of hearts? It was a process that didn't start out perfectly.

As an adult, Anna's choices led her to a bad marriage and the comfort of alcohol abuse.

After her first marriage disintegrated in the shame-filled bog of old memories, she married again and took her childhood commitment to Christ off the shelf. She and her believing husband attended church regularly, but shame of the past still haunted her present. Anna put the bottle away, plastered a big smile on her face, and joined the ranks of others who answered the question, "How are you today?" with the standard, "Fine, just fine." That was her answer because she thought that's what it was supposed to be. But she was not fine.

"Just because you become a Christian doesn't make all the pain go away," Anna told me. "I lost years of my life and couldn't get them back. That dark void left me feeling like I was in a freefall most of the time. I was surrounded by church people, but I still felt terribly alone. I was afraid to trust anyone, so I kept others at arm's length. If you tell yourself you're tall, that doesn't make you tall. If you tell yourself you're fine, that doesn't make you fine. I was a saved mess."

One day, Anna decided enough was enough. She was going to stop picking at the scab of her past and allow it to heal. She braved her way into a Celebrate Recovery meeting, told a little bit of her story, and met other brave souls who did the same. For the first time, she took the dark, hidden chapters of her story and brought them out into the light. That's when her healing began.

A few months later, she met with a trauma counselor. With the Bible in one hand and a trauma therapy degree in the other, the therapist led Anna to a place of healing and wholeness. You can't connect the dots until you gather the dots. The therapist helped Anna gather her fragmented memories and fit them together into a story that made sense. Once she decided she no longer wanted to be stuck in her bad story, Anna stopped picking at the scab of the past so it could heal. Today, she has a beautiful scar she doesn't mind showing or sharing at all.

But Anna didn't stop with her own healing. Today she is a counselor who helps other wounded souls write new endings to their stories so they can experience healing and wholeness. That is the beauty of the promise that "God causes everything [the good and the bad] to work together for the good of those who love God and are called according to his purpose for them" (Romans 8:28 NLT). Anna's story is yet another reminder that *the pages we would most likely want to remove from our story, God wants to repurpose for his glory.*

"Do you wish this wasn't your story?" I asked her.

"I don't think I would be who I am today if I had not walked through the story I had," she replied. "I would not have chosen that story, but I have no regrets. I know that God will use every bit of it to help someone else find a safe place. Nothing is ever wasted."

But is it true that nothing is ever wasted? Remember Meghan? She's the gal who constantly rehearsed her pain and refused her healing. Could the bad parts of *her* story be wasted? I believe they could. As long as she keeps picking at the scabs of past wounds, her pain will not do anybody any good—especially herself. As long as we wallow in regret and bathe in bitterness, we will remain stuck in our stories. Our worst chapters will not become our greatest victories. If we slap away God's healing hand when he reaches down, the wounds will stay just that . . . wounds.

There comes a time when we need to come to grips with what happened, forgive those who've hurt us, forgive ourselves, and move on to a new chapter.

COMING OUT OF THE SHADOWS

One of my favorite movies is *The Legend of Bagger Vance*. There is one scene that always leaves me scrambling in my purse for tissues . . . lots of tissues.

The story takes place in 1931. As a young man, Rannulph Junuh (played by Matt Damon) was a favorite son in Savannah, Georgia. An impressive golfer who showed great promise, he was the only child of a wealthy Southern family, not to mention handsome as all get out. But right in his prime, Junuh was called away to fight in World War I. During one particular battle, his entire company was killed. Junuh was the lone survivor, but he did not survive very well. Though he received the Medal of Honor, he disappeared for a time. When he finally returned home, Junuh lived as a recluse in his dilapidated family home, drinking, gambling, and feeling sorry for himself.

Through a series of events, Junuh was challenged to play in a golf tournament and represent the state of Georgia. Along with the challenge came a mysterious caddy, Bagger Vance (played by Will Smith). Bagger, as it turns out, was an angel of sorts sent to help Junuh let go of his past and move forward into his future.

In one of the final scenes, while playing in the tournament, Junuh hooks a bad left into the woods. He ventures into the quiet trees and finds his ball. Standing in the silence, his mind is transported back to the battlefield. The cacophony of war bombards him. Gunshots. Screams. Crumpled bodies. Smoky haze. Pleading eyes. He is frozen in time and can go no further.

Bagger saunters up to Junuh with a knowing look. With shaking hands and a terror-stricken face, Junuh begins to tell Bagger that he can't go on.

Junuh: I can't do this. You don't understand.

Bagger: I don't need to understand. Ain't no soul on this entire earth ain't got a burden to carry he didn't understand. You ain't alone in that. But you been carrying this one long enough. Time to go an' lay it down.

Junuh: I don't know how.

Bagger: You've got a choice. You can stop or you can start.

Junuh: Start?

Bagger: Walkin'. Right back to where you always been and then stand there. Still . . . real still . . . and remember.

Junuh: It was long ago.

Bagger: No sir. It was just a moment ago. Time for you to come on out of the shadow, Mr. Junuh. Time for you to choose.

Junuh: I can't.

Bagger: Yes, you can. But you ain't alone. I'm right here wich ya. I've been here all along. Play the game. The one that only you was meant to play. The one that was given to you when you came into the world.

Junuh takes his stance and places his hands on the club.

Bagger: Ready? Take you stance. Strike the ball, Junuh, and
don't hold nothin' back. Give it everything. Let yourself
remember . . . remember your swing. That's right. Settle
yourself. Now is the time, Junuh.

Rannulph Junuh took his stance, clutched the club, and knocked
the ball out of the woods and onto the green. He also came out of the
darkness and remembered who he was and what he was created to do.[5]

I'm no golfer, but I was standing right there in the woods with
Junuh. With sweaty palms and racing heart . . . remembering the
pain of the past . . . remembering past failures . . . remembering past
defeats . . . remembering the battles lost and the wounded left behind.

Then God came and whispered to my heart, *Don't let the memories
of the past hold you captive. I'm right here with you. I've been here all
along.*

Just as it was with Meghan and Anna, we each have a choice to let
go of or hang on to the difficult parts of our stories. Meghan and Anna
had very similar beginnings, but very different endings. I'll admit, the
decision to move toward healing can be frightening—especially if the
wounds are all we've ever known. It's easier to choose the comfort of
certainty than the unpredictability of freedom.

Like a fledgling unsure of its ability to navigate the vastness of
the open skies, we perch on the edge of the nest, wondering if we can
survive outside its safe boundaries. Something inside us tells us that we
were not made for the nest, but will we venture beyond and take flight?

Oh, my friend, I hope your answer is yes!

Take a deep breath. We're about to take two of the most important
steps on the journey. I know you can do it. God's right here with you.
He's been here all along.

Chapter Five

Changing the Ending to Your Story

Forgiveness is the key that unlocks the door
of resentment and the handcuffs of hatred.
It is a power that breaks the chains of
bitterness and the shackles of selfishness.

—Corrie ten Boom, survivor of
Ravensbrück concentration camp

Cindy longingly leafed through memories captured on brightly colored construction paper and glitter-covered popsicle sticks. Crayon-crafted rainbows. Little girl paint-stamped handprints. Pencil-scripted poems in large practiced letters. These were pieces of life that Cindy had tucked away to give her daughter, Robyn, when she grew up and had a family of her own. But that day would never come.

Bill and Cindy Griffiths led a full life with six kids in Long Island, New York. As summer began, their eldest went to work with his dad, their nine-year-old hustled off to camp, and their seven-, six-, and three-year-olds started a week of vacation Bible school. Their eleven-year-old daughter, Robyn, planned to go on a month-long road trip with Cindy's parents, Joe and Janice.

Four days into their trip, Cindy received a call from her brother, Scott. "Come home."

After the fifteen-minute drive, Cindy ran into her kitchen to find her brother looking more serious that she had ever seen him. "Cindy, there's been an accident," he said. "Dad's okay."

"And?" she demanded eyes wide.

Her brother began to cry. "Mom died"

Cindy grabbed his arms, as her voice rose, "And Robyn?"

"She died too." His voice crumbled under the weight of his words.

Cindy describes the cry that came from her soul as "a mighty force, like a volcanic eruption originating in the center of the earth. . . . ."[1] "Noooooo!" she screamed.

Bill, Cindy's husband, later wrote about his response to the news: "My thoughts flailed about in a desperate search for a thread of hope to hold onto. The threads I found were like cobwebs, vanishing at the slightest touch of reason. He wouldn't joke about something like this. His message was too simple to have been misinterpreted. He could be speaking of only one Robyn. *My Robyn.* I was getting weaker by the second from this strange weight, this pressure that seemed to be rapidly increasing all around me."[2]

Cindy's parents had pulled off the side of a lonely Nebraska road at seven thirty in the morning when a drunk driver slammed into the rear of their car. Janice and Robyn were killed on impact. There were no brake marks at the scene.

This is a bad story—a parent's worst reality. Friends and family rushed to the Griffiths' home and huddled like clumps of wilted flowers.

While Bill was angry at the woman who had killed his daughter, his greatest anger was at God. Even though he was gripped by the deepest anguish he had ever known and frustrated that no amount of rage would accomplish anything, he felt God knocking on the door of his heart and heard His quiet whisper, *I am with you*. Part of him wanted to answer, while another part did not.

He was mad at God, who could have stopped the crash but didn't. What could be the purpose of such a horrid tragedy?

Herb Vanhooser, a longtime acquaintance of the family, attended the funeral. When he walked down the corridor to a collage of photos, he said something no one else had said. One word. *"Thief."* That word resonated with Bill. The words from John 10:10 ran through his mind. "The thief comes only to steal and kill and destroy." At that moment, God opened Bill's eyes to the truth of his anger and who was ultimately responsible for that small casket in the ground.

> Until Herb said that word, my anger had been spread around. I was angry with God . . . with the drunken woman . . . my in-laws for taking Robyn on the trip . . . myself for allowing her to go. But when I heard the word *thief*, I suddenly felt I had been manipulated, like a brainless stringed puppet. Drugged with grief and despair and blinded with rage, I had focused my anger in the wrong direction.
>
> After Herb walked away, I continued to stare at the collage, his word echoing in my mind. He was right and I knew it. I knew it. The strange thing was that I had known it before Herb said anything, but the word ripped open the shutters and let in the light. Being mad at God had allowed darkness to shroud me. Everything I had been taught and had taught others about God's mercy, love, and forgiveness, I was keeping at arm's length. And that was exactly what the thief wanted.[3]

Bill knew that if he fell into the trap of blaming others, especially God, he would be stuck for the rest of his life as a stagnant likeness of the thief who robbed him of his daughter. "He whispers accusations of polluted truth and points a finger, and he delights the most when fingers are pointed at everyone but him . . . Anger and bitterness consume all of life."[4]

So Bill made a decision—a decision to forgive. He was not going to stay stuck in this part of the story but reach for healing.

> Would I go to bed with the devil and perpetuate this cycle of bitterness by focusing my wrath on a woman running from her own pain, or my in-laws, who were only seeking their granddaughter's company and happiness, or myself, for not being a more protective father? *No! No! No!* If the devil was my real enemy—and he is—then I would not shoot at his targets. I would set my sights on him and forgive them all.[5]

Cindy's road to healing was littered with potholes of pain and hairpin turns of changing emotions. As the weeks after the accident turned into months, she wondered about Verma Harrison—the woman driving the van that crashed into her parents' car. *What caused her to be in so much pain that she would be in that condition so early in the morning? How was she coping with her own nightmare? Does she know God loves her?* Many were shocked when they learned that five months after losing her mother and daughter, Cindy had written a letter of forgiveness to the woman who took their lives.

"I am not going to hold the offense against the offender . . . I am going to 'give' the offender, the debtor, the freedom from owing me. In doing so, in giving up my right to punish, I also inevitably give up any hold that the aforementioned taskmasters have on me, and I, too, and set free. . . . I am freed from the inevitable weight that resentment brings."[6] (To read Cindy's letter to Verma, visit www.sharonjaynes.com/cindyandverma.)

FORGIVENESS: WHAT IT IS
AND WHAT IT IS NOT

The Greek word for *forgiveness* used in the New Testament is *aphiemi*, and it means "to let go from one's power, possession, to let go free, let escape."[7] It conjures the image of forgiveness as cutting someone loose. Imagine that the perpetrator (the unforgiven) is roped to the back of the victim (the unforgiving). When we refuse to forgive, we bind ourselves to the person who has wounded us. When we forgive, we cut the person loose from our backs and set *ourselves* free.

Forgiveness can also be understood as canceling a debt. Not just canceling the debt as if it never occurred but taking the loss and refusing to make the offender pay it back. When we forgive someone, we absorb the cost of the wrong. All forgiveness is costly. Consider the price Jesus paid to absorb our debt of sin. With forgiveness comes a death of sorts—a death to the desire for revenge or payback. And with *that* death comes resurrection—a new birth of grace and freedom.

In the Old Testament, when someone paid a debt, a notice of the debt paid in full was nailed to the lender's door. That is what Jesus did when he was nailed to the cross—the debt for our sin was paid in full and nailed to heaven's door.

It's a natural response to want someone to pay for a wrong. That's why we mentally lock offenders in debtors' prison and throw away the key until they offer an acceptable apology or show adequate remorse, even though that isn't likely to ever happen. When we hang on to the hurt and refuse to let it go, we essentially share a jail cell with the offender, which means neither of us is free. However, when we forgive someone, we cancel a debt—which the other person could never repay anyway—and then both of us are free.

Forgiveness has nothing to do with whether or not the offender deserves forgiveness. I do not deserve God's forgiveness, and yet he has forgiven me. It is not saying that what the person did or didn't do doesn't matter. If it didn't matter, there would be nothing to forgive. It is no longer allowing the offender to hold *you* captive by holding a grudge. You forgive the offender not because he or she deserves it, but because you need it.

We can hate an act but choose not to hate the person who committed it. I am sure that Bill and Cindy Griffiths still hate what Verma Harrison did, even though they do not hate Verma herself. Corrie ten Boom, a Nazi concentration camp survivor, once said, "Forgiveness is the key that unlocks the handcuffs of hate."

Bill and Cindy understood that forgiveness is a door we have to walk through for healing to take place. If we refuse to cross the threshold, we'll remain stuck in the bad chapters of our stories and unable to move forward to write better ones.

For the longest time, I felt that the person who wounded me in the worst way should at least have to ask for forgiveness. Then I realized that when Jesus cried out his final words on the cross, "Father, forgive them for they don't know what they are doing," the people who crucified him hadn't asked at all. He forgave them when even they didn't realize they needed it.

Biblical forgiveness is not transactional—we don't give forgiveness with the expectation of getting something back. That means forgiveness is always a one-way proposition, whether or not the offender acknowledges the offense. The choice to forgive is independent of the offender's involvement.

THE HIGHER STEP

It was a Saturday college football game and I was doing what I like doing best—not watching the game but observing people. My seat was on the end of a long row of Carolina blue bleachers, and I had a steady flow of fans walking past me up and down the concrete steps for two and a half hours. After a while, I noticed that four out of five people walking up the stands tripped on the step right in front of me and to my left. At halftime, I measured and discovered that the step was about a quarter-inch higher than the others. So, the people tripped.

Forgiveness is like that step. It's just a little bit higher than anything else we're going to talk about in these pages. Unfortunately, it's the one step a lot of us seem to trip on the most. But we can do it. Just pick up those determined feet a little bit higher, and let's keep going.

The high step of forgiveness is at the very core of the Christian faith and a foundational theme in Jesus' teachings. Here are just a few examples:

"And when you stand praying, if you hold anything against anyone, forgive them, so that your Father in heaven may forgive you your sins." (Mark 11:25)

"For if you forgive other people when they sin against you, your heavenly Father will also forgive you. But if you do not forgive others their sins, your Father will not forgive your sins." (Matthew 6:14–15)

When Jesus was with the disciples at the last supper, he offered them wine and said,

"This is my blood of the covenant, which is poured out for many for the forgiveness of sins." (Matthew 26:28)

Throughout Old Testament times, God's people offered sacrifices for the forgiveness of their sins, but their sacrifices were never enough—every new sin required another sacrifice. Jesus died as the final sacrifice for the forgiveness of our sins. His sacrifice was enough. I love how author and pastor Brian Zahnd described Jesus' forgiveness as "grace that takes the blame, covers the shame, and removes the stain and the endless cycle of revenge."[8]

But we aren't merely recipients of forgiving grace through Jesus' sacrifice on the cross; we are also called to be givers of that forgiving grace. As C. S. Lewis said, "To be Christian means to forgive the inexcusable, because God has forgiven the inexcusable in you."[9]

In teaching his followers to forgive, Jesus identified no exceptions—no loopholes that let us off the hook from forgiving. He mentioned no crime too heinous, no abuse too perverse, no act too vile to warrant holding on to unforgiveness. Just yesterday, I received a letter from a man on death row. He had beaten his brother to death. "Can God forgive even me?" he asked. Yes, he can.

Brian Zahnd once wrote a formal response to the question of whether or not a repentant war criminal—a Nazi who had committed heinous acts—could be forgiven. In commenting on his response, he said, "I'm convinced that if forgiveness is impossible for a repentant war criminal simply because his sins are too terrible, then the Christian gospel is a fairy tale, and we might as well abandon the charade." He went on to say, "Christian forgiveness is not cheap. Rather it is costly because it flows from the cross."[10]

When we make the costly choice to forgive, we not only live out a foundational tenet of our faith but also put a stop to the endless cycle of revenge, releasing the burden of bitterness, and making the world beautiful through grace.

LOOKING INTO THE FACE OF GOD

Jacob. Now, there's a biblical patriarch who has quite a story when it comes to forgiveness. He and his momma grabbed the pen right out of God's hand, as if God needed help writing their story. While Jacob's mother, Rebekah, was pregnant, God told her:

> Two nations are in your womb,
>   and two peoples from within you will be separated;
>   one people will be stronger than the other,
>   and the older will serve the younger. (Genesis 25:23)

Rebekah did indeed give birth to two very unidentical twin brothers—hairy Esau and smooth Jacob. The name Jacob means "heel grabber." The boys wrestled in the womb, and Jacob, though born second, came out hanging on to his older brother's heel. That might have been a fun story to tell at a party if Jacob hadn't continued to try to gain one-upmanship on Esau. Unfortunately for Esau, the name Jacob also means "deceiver, supplanter, or usurper."

As the boys grew into young men, Esau was a ruddy man's man, a skilled hunter, and an outdoorsman. Jacob was a momma's boy who preferred staying inside and cooking stew. Isaac loved Esau. Rebekah loved Jacob. That's a setup for the boys to be at odds with each other from the very beginning.

Being the firstborn meant Esau would receive the birthright and the blessing. The birthright was a double portion of the inheritance. The blessing referred to the transfer of authority, leadership, and ultimate prosperity from father to son. Jacob knew that. Jacob wanted that.

One day, Esau came home famished after a day of hunting. He smelled Jacob's stew wafting through the house and asked him for a bowl. Jacob said, "Sure, but sell me your birthright first." Jacob wanted the birthright. Jacob got the birthright. Now on to the blessings.

God had already told Rebekah that the younger would rule the elder, but apparently, she felt God needed her help to make that happen. So, she came up with a plan.

When Isaac was very old and nearly blind, it was time to give his eldest son the blessing. Rebekah was not going to let that happen. She convinced Jacob to cover his arms with goat hair and pretend to be

Esau. When he presented himself to his father, Isaac fell for the ruse and gave Jacob the blessing that belonged to Esau. When Esau learned of the deception, he begged his father to renege and reverse the oath. When Isaac wouldn't, or rather couldn't, Esau vowed to kill his brother. "Esau held a grudge against Jacob because of the blessing his father had given him. He said to himself, 'The days of mourning for my father are near; then I will kill my brother Jacob'" (27:41). Another translation says that "Esau hated Jacob" because he stole the blessing (NLT).

The Hebrew word translated *grudge* means "to cherish animosity against."[11] I doubt many would admit that they *cherish* the hate they have toward another, but it's easy to do. You take care of what you cherish. Dust it off. Shine it up. Hold it dear. Unforgiveness sits as a beloved trophy on the shelf of the heart.

For the next twenty-one years, Jacob hid from his angry brother as a fugitive in Haran. He accumulated wives, children, flocks, servants, and great wealth while living with his father-in-law, Laban. But eventually, Jacob decided he wanted to return to his homeland and his people. There was just one problem—Esau, who had vowed to kill him.

When Jacob left Laban and headed toward his homeland, angels of God met him along the road. "This is the camp of God!" he exclaimed at their appearance. So he named the place "Mahanaim," which means two camps (Genesis 32:1–2).

Jacob's strategy for dealing with Esau was to divide his people and possessions into two groups or two camps. One was to approach Esau first. If Esau and his four hundred men attacked and killed the first group, then the second would flee. If Esau didn't kill the first group, then the second would proceed.

When the first group approached Esau, rather than attack them, he ran to embrace them. The same happened with the second group. When Jacob brought up the rear, a teary-eyed Esau embraced his brother and wept. Just the night before, Jacob had been preparing for the worst, but in the morning he was met with Esau's best. Esau embraced his brother, offering forgiveness and inviting reconciliation.

Jacob said to Esau, "To see your face is like seeing the face of God, now that you have received me favorably" (33:10).

Seeing forgiveness face-to-face is like seeing the face of God. Isn't that the most beautiful image? If we were sitting together sharing a cup of coffee, I'd want to chat long about that. Can you think of a time when someone forgave you and it felt as if you were looking into the face of God? I have. We are never more like God than when we forgive.

The word *Mahanaim* would forever remind the Israelite nation of a time when a crossfire of animosity became a ceasefire of peace, a time when the story of God's people took a radical change of direction. After many years of hostility, Jacob and Esau reunited with tears and dancing. The name Mahanaim subsequently also came to refer to a Hebrew dance of reconciliation (Song of Solomon 6:13). It's a dance we can all learn, moving to the rhythm of forgiveness and the tune of grace.

> *Seeing forgiveness face-to-face is like seeing the face of God.*

Interestingly, the night before Jacob came face-to-face with Esau, he wrestled with a "man" many scholars believe to be the preincarnate Christ. In the heat of the struggle, Jacob declared, "I will not let you go unless you bless me" (Genesis 32:26). Bless his heart, he now realized that a stolen blessing was no blessing at all.

> "What is your name?" the man asked.
>
> He replied, "Jacob."
>
> "Your name will no longer be Jacob," the man told him. "From now on you will be called Israel, because you have fought with God and with men and have won." (vv. 27–28 NLT)

The name Jacob means "trickster," but the name Israel means "triumphant with God." Jacob's worst chapter was about to become his greatest victory.

REFLECTING THE FACE OF GOD

I'm going to backtrack a bit here in Jacob's story, because sometimes we have to look backward in order to move forward. All those years ago, Esau was devastated to learn that Jacob had tricked their father into giving him the birthright and the blessing. Picture the scene:

> Esau pleaded, "But do you have only one blessing? Oh my father, bless me, too!" Then Esau broke down and wept.
>
> Finally, his father, Isaac, said to him,
>
> "You will live away from the richness of the earth,
> and away from the dew of the heaven above.
> You will live by your sword,
> and you will serve your brother.
> *But when you decide to break free,*
> you will shake his yoke from your neck."
>
> (27:38–40 NLT, emphasis added)

We don't know much about what went on with Esau between the time his brother fled to Haran and the time Jacob returned home to Bethel. We do know that Esau did not like his story. But something happened in Esau's heart over those twenty years. He went from vowing to kill his brother to embracing him when he returned. I'm sure it was a process, but it started with a decision.

Let's go back and look at Isaac's words to Esau: "But when you *decide* to break free, you will shake his yoke from your neck" (v. 40 NLT, emphasis added). In other translations, Isaac says, "But when you grow restless, you will throw his yoke from off your neck," and "when you will grow restive and break loose, and you shall tear his yoke from off your neck" (NIV and AMPC).

The Hebrew word translated "break loose" in the Amplified Bible is *paraq*, which also means "deliver or rescue."[12] When do we break loose from the yoke of unforgiveness that wraps around our necks and weighs on our shoulders? When we get restless and *decide* to break free of the bondage. That's when our stories will take a new direction.

I can assure you of this, the devil does not want you to break free from the weight of the past. He wants you to wear that yoke of bitterness and resentment for the rest of your life. I can envision him polishing the yoke with a fresh coat of remembrance so shiny he can see his reflection in the surface. Paul wrote, "I have forgiven in the sight of Christ for your sake, in order that Satan might not outwit us. For we are not unaware of his schemes" (2 Corinthians 2:10–11). And what are these schemes? To keep you stuck in a bad story on a dog-eared page of unforgiveness. What is God's ultimate best? To set you free from the burden of resentment so you can write a new ending to your story.

It was Esau's decision to forgive that set both brothers free from the hate place. Esau was free, and he set Jacob free as well. At the time of Jacob's betrayal, I'm sure Esau thought he could never forgive the offense. But grace takes what is impossible with man and makes it possible with God.

"UNHUMANABLE" GRACE

Mark and Jill met on a blind date and were engaged three months later. Jill was raised in an emotionally healthy Christian home, while

Mark came from an emotionally dysfunctional environment. Shortly after the wedding, Mark enrolled in seminary and Jill's stick turned blue. Twenty-seven years later, Mark was pastoring a growing church, Jill was leading an international ministry, and they had five children. Life was good . . . or so it seemed.

After twenty-seven years, Mark felt like he needed a break from the stresses of leading a church. He resigned his position as senior pastor and started a construction company. On one hand, Mark was relieved to be free of the pressures of ministry; on the other hand, he felt a loss of self-worth and value in doing so.

Mark had always struggled with depression. It wasn't a constant battle, but the dark cloud came and went with the winds of time. A year after he started his business, Mark began a downward spiral that took him to a dark place he had never been before. It was during this time that Jill discovered a string of text messages on Mark's cell phone. He had reconnected with an old girlfriend on Facebook and was having an affair.

Disbelief. Devastation. Jarring emotions. Spiritual whiplash. There just weren't enough words to describe how Jill felt at the moment of discovery.

Mark continued living at home for six excruciating months after Jill confronted him about the affair. Then one day, he packed his bags and headed off into his new life. "I'm filing for divorce," he announced. "I'm done here."

Jill, like most spouses who make such a discovery, was in shock. The betrayal sucker-punched her and left her gasping for air. Her brain was foggy, her emotions ragged, and her body just about shut down. Fortunately, Jill had a strong community of three friends who became her stretcher bearers. She had three teens still at home, and her friends kept the house running when she couldn't.

One night, Jill lay flat on the floor and cried out to God. "I don't know what to do! God, tell me what to do!" Then words that were not her own filled her mind. *Love him.* That is not what Jill wanted to hear. Again, the words echoed, *Love him.*

Jill knew the words were from God, and she didn't like it. Loving Mark was the last thing on her mind. She got up off the floor, raised her fist toward God, and shouted, "I don't want to do this! This is too hard! He is not lovable!"

And then a balm washed over her when she heard God's response. *Yes, Jill. And sometimes you aren't lovable either.*

"You're right," she prayed. "You love me when I am not lovable. But I don't know how to love him like that. I don't even like him. You'll have to show me." A passage from Romans that described love in action became God's answer and her anchor (12:9–12). "Love must be sincere," it began. "Hate what is evil; cling to what is good. . . . Be joyful in hope, patient in affliction, faithful in prayer." She read it every day. Again, and again, and again. Those verses became her marching orders. Instead of lashing out, Jill met Mark's kick in the gut with kindness.

Nine months after Jill discovered Mark's affair, he asked her, "Why are you treating me so kindly when I've treated you so poorly?"

"I don't know," she replied. "It's unhumanable."

"What does that mean?" he asked.

"I don't know," she said. "I just made it up." *Unhumanable* was the only word she could think of to convey that her kindness wasn't humanly possible.

Four months after Mark packed his bags and drove away to his new life, he had an encounter with God. It was on an Easter Sunday, and he experienced his own resurrection.

After Mark's encounter with God, Jill saw a level of surrender, sadness, and contrition she had never seen before. He truly repented and longed to come back home. Jill eventually said he could. "I didn't trust him yet," she said. "That had to be earned with right behavior over a period of time. But I was willing to forgive him."

It is that last sentence that conveys what Jill described as "unhumanable." And it is. Forgiveness is divine. Forgiveness is the salve God used to heal the wound of a marriage flayed open by betrayal and stitched together with threads of grace. It was forgiveness that changed the ending to Jill's story. Her worst chapter became her greatest victory—and it started with an unhumanable decision.

WHEN THE STORY HAS A DIFFERENT ENDING

Perhaps you're reading Jill's story and thinking, *Good for her. But my story didn't have a happy ending. There was no reconciliation. There was no restoration. There was no repentant heart made new. My life broke and the pieces still lie scattered.*

What about the tear-smudged ink on divorce papers and the ache in *that* heart? How does forgiveness change the ending to *that* story? Here's some good news: just because *the marriage* broke doesn't mean *you* have to stay broken.

At the same time Jill was struggling with Mark's betrayal, another friend of mine was experiencing a similar betrayal. We'll call her Angela, and her husband Mike. Angela and Mike were both believers and committed to having a Christian marriage. Angela was drawn to Mike's gentleness and even-keeled personality. He was a good provider and an attentive father to their three children. However, Mike was never very affectionate with Angela and always seemed to keep physical intimacy at arm's length.

Eventually, Mike took a job that required a one-hour commute. He worked incessantly and was always exhausted. Angela initiated many conversations about how they weren't connecting emotionally or physically, but Mike just shrugged it off. "I've got deadlines," he said. "This is what it takes to succeed. Get used to it."

After a while, Mike began pulling all-nighters at the office. After several all-nighters, Angela grew suspicious. It was then that her sister discovered a Facebook page with posts of Mike and a much younger woman—a woman who had previously been arrested for solicitation. Over the following weeks, more layers of Mike's sexual activities were exposed.

Like Jill, Angela was in shock. There weren't enough tears to wash away the pain. Like Jill, Angela prayed, sought wise counsel, and tried to love Mike back to the marriage. Unlike Jill, Angela's husband did not come home. After thirty-five years of marriage, the divorce was finalized.

So, what is Angela supposed to do with that? How does she forgive when the chapter doesn't have a happy ending? I asked my sweet friend how she was coping with the loss.

"I'm still coming to terms with what is now my life," she said. "This isn't how I thought I'd end up. There are layers and layers of grief I'm having to work through. I get through one, and then something happens, and I go through another one. There's the loss of companionship, the loss of the family unit, and the loss of trust. I had a great relationship with God before this happened, but now it's on steroids. I depend on God for every breath.

"From the very beginning, I decided that I was not going to allow bitterness, anger, or resentment to rule or ruin my life. I forgave Mike for what he did. That doesn't mean that I would put myself in harm's way or pretend the betrayal didn't happen, but I have forgiven him. How could I not? Look how God has forgiven me. His grace has no limits. I'm prepared to move on, even though I'm not sure what that looks like, but I trust God. He knows what's around every corner."

This chapter of Angela's story didn't end with God's repairing the broken pieces and handing back the marriage with a shiny bow. But it did end with Angela feeling that God was repairing *her* and giving her the strength to move forward. It wasn't a storybook ending, but it was a redemptive one. She no longer feels broken, and she has a new story to tell about how God has brought her through.

THE GOOD ENDING TO A BAD STORY

Let's go back to Cindy, Bill, and Verma's tragic story at the beginning of the chapter. After Cindy sent her grace-filled, gospel-saturated letter of forgiveness to Verma, the story pivoted on mercy and those who chose to give it. In the months following the accident, Verma pulled the blinds, sequestered in her basement, and stared at the ceiling beams thinking how easy it would be to get a rope and end it all. However, Verma is quick to say that it was Cindy's words of forgiveness that leapt from the page, and kept her from taking her own life. On the day of Verma's sentencing, the judge was ready to lock her up for two counts of involuntary manslaughter . . . until he read Cindy's letter. Because of the Griffiths' request, the judge sentenced Verma to probation with random drug and alcohol testing.

"I can tell you," Verma wrote to Cindy, "if it weren't for your forgiveness and love, I wouldn't be alive. If it weren't for your beautiful letter, I wouldn't be home with my babies; I would not even know God." Amazingly, more than twenty years later, these two women are inexplicably bound in friendship: the forgiver and the forgiven.

I met Cindy while speaking at a conference in New York and saw the tangled confluence that the pain and purpose of a new ending brings. Janice and Robyn are still gone. But because of forgiveness, neither Bill, Cindy, nor Verma remains stuck in a story of resentment, anger, or shame. They each have a redemptive story that would never have happened without the giving and receiving of God's grace. The resurrection power of Jesus transformed the worst chapter of their lives into one of their greatest victories in the battle between love and hate, good and evil, past pain and present purpose.

Chapter Six

Leaving the Shame Place

Hardships often prepare ordinary
people for extraordinary destiny.

—C. S. Lewis, *The Voyage of the Dawn Treader*

Pat flipped through tattered magazines in the dark, dank reception room of a questionable medical facility. She had never been to this part of town with topless bars, strip clubs, and pawnshops lining the streets. The office was tucked in a strip mall between a laundromat and a bail bonds office. The black bars on the windows resembled a prison cell more than a doctor's office. The musty scent of mildew mixed with antiseptic assaulted her senses and made her feel dirty. *This doesn't feel right,* Pat mused. *I don't need to stoop this low. It's not like I'm doing anything wrong. I deserve better.*

Pat was raised in a nice home with a mom and dad who loved her. Church wasn't a big part of their lives, but they did attend on holidays such as Easter and Christmas. When she was sixteen, she decided to marry her high school sweetheart. No amount of cajoling or reasoning could convince her to wait until she and her boyfriend were older. After the wedding, it wasn't too long before the young bride discovered she was pregnant, and the family of three moved in with her parents in Tampa, Florida. A few months later, Pat's teenaged husband packed up his meager belongings and stole away in the middle of the night, leaving Pat to raise their son on her own. From his new California address, he made little contact and closed that chapter of his life with the words, "Thanks, but no thanks."

Full of grace, Pat's parents helped her through high school and eventually college. They set her and her son up in an apartment, paid her tuition, and babysat when they could. Even though her young life was littered with poor choices, Pat was determined to become a strong and independent businesswoman who lived life on her own terms. *Who needs a husband anyway?* she thought.

On the first day of college, while standing in a registration line, Pat eyed a handsome ex-marine with salt-and-pepper hair who was assisting new students. Her heart flip-flopped in her chest, but she kept her determined eyes focused on the task at hand. However, when they ran in to each other a few weeks later, her protective walls collapsed as she gazed into the blue of his eyes. His muscular build and premature gray hair gave him the aura of both stability and maturity—a stark contrast to her high school relationship. A few days later, their romance began with a flash. No warmup. No buildup. Simply two people lovestruck.

Several months into the relationship, Pat knew she was pregnant.

"I had already done this one time," she explained. "Even though I loved my four-year-old son, I didn't want another child right then. Mike and I were engaged. I didn't want to start a marriage already pregnant, but with as little baggage as possible. Besides, I was going to be a career woman, and another child didn't fit into my plans to start my own insurance agency. So, I decided to have an abortion."

Mike was somewhat stunned and silenced with this new turn of events. Pat simply told him she was going to have an abortion. Period. She didn't want anyone to know, especially her parents. Mike felt he didn't have any say-so in the matter, so he just kept quiet.

And that's how she ended up sitting in the dimly lit abortion clinic in the middle of a strip mall. Barred windows. Barred heart. Mildewed carpet. Made-up mind. If Pat could rewrite her story, this is where she would tear out the tear-stained pages and insert new ones with fresh ink and unmarred edges. But she can't. So, let's keep going.

A darkness hovered low as Pat waited in that reception room. The barricaded windows cast distorted lines on the threadbare carpet. Something felt wrong. "I didn't allow the feeling that the decision was wrong to change my mind about having an abortion. Instead, I changed my mind about *where* I would have an abortion. *I deserve better than this,* I thought. *I don't need to hide in some seedy abortion clinic. It's my right to have this procedure performed in a clean medical facility by a professional staff. Yes, I have the right to a nice and easy abortion.* After all, she had written her first published paper in college on a woman's right to choose.

Pat picked up her purse and left the abortion clinic. With one phone call, she scheduled a consultation with her regular Ob-Gyn. The pristine doctor's office stood in stark contrast to the dingy abortion clinic. Cheery lighting, crisp décor, and a professional staff gave her a sense of safety and security.

"The consultation wasn't much of a consultation at all," Pat shared with me. "The emotionless, automaton gynecologist didn't ask me any questions and I didn't offer any information. He didn't ask me why I wanted an abortion; he barely looked me in the eye. The doctor didn't tell me how far along I was or what the procedure entailed. He just told me to show up at 7:00 a.m. on the day of the procedure and I'd be out in time for lunch. It would be all over in thirty minutes, and I could get back to life as usual. 'Think of it like a three-hour break in your busy day,' he said. 'No big deal.'"

But it was a big deal.

Pat and Mike got married two weeks before the scheduled abortion, but the honeymoon wasn't what they had hoped. As they lay in each other's arms, another life lay between them . . . a life they tried to ignore. What should have been the happiest time of their lives was the union of two broken people filled with shame, self-loathing, and sharp places that raked across each other's souls.

On the day of the abortion, Pat opted to have general anesthesia rather than local—she wanted to be completely sedated and unaware of what was going on. With a mask securely fastened over her mouth and nose, she closed her eyes and drifted into twilight. However, when she awoke, it wasn't to the sounds of a post-op nurse clearing the room, but the swooshing sound of a respirator pumping oxygen into her lungs. She couldn't move her body or speak past the intubation tube running down her throat. *Where am I? Why can't I speak?* Within moments, she wished she hadn't awakened at all.

When her eyes finally focused, she saw her distraught parents at the foot of the bed and a tear-stained husband holding her feet, all of them willing her to wake up.

Once Pat regained consciousness, the doctor came in to explain the situation. "You had an allergic reaction to the anesthetic," he said. "When you stopped breathing, we had to put you on a respirator with a tube down your throat to keep you alive. You've been unconscious for six hours." Her goal had been to have the simple procedure without her parents knowing about it. Now they did.

Over the next few days, Pat developed a high fever, nausea, vomiting, and excruciating pain. The doctor's office told her not to worry about it but to take some ibuprofen. A trip back to the doctor's office five days later revealed the problem.

"During the emergency procedure from your first abortion attempt," the doctor began, "parts of the fetus were left behind. We'll have to do the abortion over again to remove them."

The word *fetus* sucker-punched Pat in the gut. For the very first time, she allowed herself to see this pregnancy not as a condition, but as a baby—her baby. Her mind spun out of control and she felt as though she were going to pass out. *Parts were left behind? What parts? Arms? Legs? Heart? Oh God, what parts?* In one moment, Pat went from being a brave woman in charge of her destiny to a shame-filled little girl out of control.

After the second procedure, neither she nor Mike ever mentioned the abortion again. Shame had silenced them both. The secret was filed away in the cold metal drawer of a doctor's office between K and M. Pat and Mike had another son a few years later, but by that time, the marriage was little more than a cauldron of anger, bitterness, and resentment. One day, Pat drove home from her insurance agency, swung her 280Z sports car into the driveway, and walked her stiletto-clad feet into their fashionable home. "It's over, Mike," she said. "I'm done. Get out." Shame had won . . . temporarily.

THE DEFINING CHARACTERISTICS OF SHAME

We're going to leave Pat's story for just a moment to take a closer look at shame, which is one of the most heartrending reasons many of us don't like our stories.

In the previous chapter, we looked at the importance of forgiving others. *But what if the person you need to forgive is yourself?* I often hear people say, "I know God forgives me, but I can't forgive myself." This is where shame comes in. To refuse God's forgiveness is to step under a cloud of shame, which is a place God never intended us to be. Refusing to forgive ourselves and living in shame are one and the same. Just as forgiving others sets us free from the hate place, forgiving ourselves sets us free from the shame place.

What exactly is shame?

Scholar and psychologist Gershen Kaufman said, "Shame is the most disturbing experience individuals ever have about themselves; no other emotion feels more deeply disturbing because in the moment of shame the self feels wounded from within."[1]

Shame isn't just a feeling that you have *done* something wrong, but a sense that you *are* something wrong. It is the intensely painful belief that you are damaged beyond repair and therefore unworthy of love and acceptance. Shame is a deep-seated belief that you are irreversibly flawed because of past failures, mistakes, abuses, or misuses. It serves as a zoom lens that tightens the view so that all you see are your faults. As long as you and I remain under the cloud of shame, we will never have a better story or experience the victory in it. That's why it's so important to find our way out.

> *Just as forgiving others sets us free from the hate place, forgiving ourselves sets us free from the shame place.*

Some confuse shame and embarrassment; however, the two are very different. Embarrassment is what we feel for a moment when we accidentally burp at a dinner party, walk out of a public restroom with toilet paper stuck to our shoe, or call a friend by the wrong name. Embarrassment is temporary and doesn't have lasting effects on our life. Embarrassing stories are often humorous. Shameful stories never are.

Guilt is another experience that is often confused with shame. *Merriam-Webster* defines guilt as "responsibility for having done something wrong and especially something against the law." It defines shame as "a painful emotion caused by consciousness of guilt, shortcoming, or impropriety; a condition of humiliating disgrace or disrepute." Did you catch the differences between the two? Guilt is a feeling. Shame is a feeling that leads to a condition.

The experience of guilt and shame may feel the same for a moment, but they lead us to different conclusions. We feel guilty because of what we've done; we feel ashamed because of who we are. Guilt says, "I made a mistake." Shame says, "I am a mistake."

Healthy guilt is necessary to lead a healthy life. It can lead to confession: "I am sorry for what I've done. Will you please forgive me?" The positive outcome of dealing with guilt is that it prompts us to pursue restitution or reconciliation. It causes us to run to God and ask for his forgiveness—or at least it should. If we don't carry our guilt to God so it can be removed, that guilt can carry us into shame where it remains.

Shame happens when we internalize what has been done to us and through us, and hide it. Now we have a secret, and the silence leads to soul-seclusion and self-degradation. It makes us think the failure or abuse is who we are rather than what we did or what was done to us. Shame is more likely to lead to self-destructive behavior because shame-filled souls feel they can never change and are getting what they deserve. Author and researcher Brené Brown said, "Shame is the intensely painful feeling or experience of believing we are flawed and therefore unworthy of acceptance and belonging."[2] The shame-shackled heart concludes, "I am sorry for who I am. I'm a bad person." We fear people won't like us if they knew the truth about where we've come from or what we've done. It makes us feel that we are small, damaged, and never enough.

Shame can sink its claws into us even when we can't put our finger on where it came from or what caused it. I remember as a little girl, hiding under the covers of my bed, trying to shut out my parents' yelling and screaming in the next room. I heard bad words. I didn't know what some of them meant, but I did know how they made me feel. Dirty. The next morning, I awoke to the aftermath of the night's tirade—Mom's black eye, Dad's crying remorse, furniture tossed and broken, glass smashed and scattered—and those bad words bouncing around my little-girl head.

Nevertheless, I was expected to put on my school clothes, brush my hair, eat my cereal, brush my teeth, and sit in class with my little friends as if nothing had happened the night before. The shame of what I'd seen and heard clung to me like the stink of a Friday night fish fry. Maybe no one else could smell it, but I sure did. Never once did I wonder what went on in anyone else's home. I was sure it couldn't be as bad as mine. Shame wrapped its talons around my neck and squeezed. I hadn't done anything wrong, but I felt I was wrong. My family was all wrong. And I suffered in silence.

Whether it attacks a curly-headed first-grader sitting at her desk or an eighty-year-old woman sitting in a church pew with her friends, shame is a universal destroyer of destinies, dignity, and callings. It whispers, *You're the only one. No one is as bad as you. If they only knew.* Shame keeps its victims silent.

THE ORIGINS OF SHAME

Where did shame come from? How did it creep into the world? We have to go all the way back to Genesis 3 to answer that question. In chapter 2, we talked about how there was no shame when God created the heavens and the earth. There was no shame when he reached down, gathered a holy handful of dust, and formed the first man in his own image. There was no shame when God took one of Adam's ribs and fashioned Eve to be Adam's companion and completer. There was no shame when God placed the couple in the garden to rule over all he had created and be fruitful and multiply. After the second creation account in Genesis 2, the chapter closes with the words, "Adam and his wife were both naked, and they felt no shame" (v. 25).

The biblical writer could have used a variety of words to describe what Adam and Eve *did not* feel. They felt no fear, no hunger, no anxiety, no thirst, no loneliness, no lack. But the writer chose the word *shame*. It's a significant choice as it foreshadows what happened next.

> When the woman saw that the fruit of the tree was good for food
> and pleasing to the eye, and also desirable for gaining wisdom, she
> took some and ate it. She also gave some to her husband, who was
> with her, and he ate it. Then the eyes of both of them were opened,
> and they realized they were naked; so they sewed fig leaves together
> and made coverings for themselves. (3:6–7)

The Hebrew word for shame is *bosh*, which means to be "utterly dejected and to be ashamed in front of one another."[3] After they ate the forbidden fruit, Adam and Eve immediately tried to cover their shame by sewing fig leaves together to make aprons. I imagine Satan looked at their uncovered backsides and laughed as they walked away. When aprons weren't enough, they tried hiding from God among the trees of the garden. But that didn't work either.

"Where are you?" God called to the crouching couple. It wasn't that God didn't know where they were, but he wanted them to admit what they had done. That's always the first step toward coming out from under the shadow of shame that results from sin. Where are you? What have you done? Say it. Name it.

While Eve was the first to speak up when questioned by the serpent, Adam was the first to speak up when questioned by God.

> He [Adam] answered, "I heard you in the garden, and I was afraid
> because I was naked; so I hid."
> And he [God] said, "Who told you that you were naked? Have
> you eaten from the tree that I commanded you not to eat from?"
> The man said, "The woman you put here with me—she gave
> me some fruit from the tree, and I ate it."

Then the LORD God said to the woman, "What is this you have done?"

The woman said, "The serpent deceived me, and I ate." (vv. 10–13)

Adam initially blamed Eve, but ultimately blamed God: "The woman *you* put here with me—she gave me some fruit from the tree, and I ate it." In other words, *If you had not given me this woman, none of this would have happened.* How many times have I, have you, blamed God for the consequences of our own poor choices?

Then Eve blamed the serpent: "The serpent deceived me, and I ate" (v. 13).

So, Adam blamed Eve. Eve blamed the serpent. And the serpent just laughed.

Did you notice that neither Adam nor Eve actually answered God's question, "Who told you that you were naked?" No one had to tell them. They knew because shame told them.

Looking back to Adam and Eve, we can see how what started in the garden continues to manifest itself in our own lives today.

- Shame hides authenticity.
- Shame denies responsibility.
- Shame blames vehemently.
- Shame blocks vulnerability.
- Shame breeds insecurity.
- Shame destroys dignity.
- Shame shackles us to our past.
- Shame keeps our stories stuck in the worst chapters, blocking our ability to move forward into better ones.

From the first time shame entered the world until today, it has looked the same, felt the same, and had the same effect on all humankind. What we see in the garden of Eden, we also see when we look in the mirror.

Don't you just love the fact that the first question recorded in the Bible is God asking, "Where are you?" Our heavenly Father still asks that question. When we want to hide in shame, he calls to us, "Where are you?" Even in the shame of our own making he pursues us, longing to restore the rent relationship.

GOD'S CURE FOR SHAME

God didn't leave the first man and woman helpless or hopeless with the infection of shame. He called Adam and Eve out of hiding, confronted their disobedience, and covered their naked skin with animal skin. This is the first mention of death in the Bible, and it came as God sacrificed an animal to cover human shame. The sacrifice was a foreshadowing of the ultimate sacrifice God would make to cover our sin once and for all—the sacrifice of Jesus on the cross. Interestingly, linguistic studies say the root of the word *shame* is thought to derive from an older word meaning "to cover," such as covering oneself literally or figuratively.[4] When we go back to Genesis 3, we see that's exactly what it means.

The animal slain for Adam and Eve's sin provided only a temporary covering, as did all the animal sacrifices that filled the pages of the Old Testament. From Genesis 3 through Malachi 4, God's people offered one sacrifice after another, and it was never enough. God knew that. He had another plan.

At just the right time on God's kingdom calendar, he sent his Son, Jesus, to earth in the form of a baby. Jesus was both fully God and fully human, something our finite minds cannot understand. Jesus lived a perfect, sinless life, and then he gave himself as a sacrifice for our sin—he paid the price to set us free so we could get out from under the tyranny of shame. Jesus was the final sacrifice, given once for all (Hebrews 10:1–18). The prophet Isaiah hauntingly said, "It was the LORD's good plan to crush him and cause him grief" (Isaiah 53:10 NLT). God loves us that much. Jesus' sacrifice ended the need for any other sacrifices.

When shame is a result of sin, the Bible gives us this promise: "If we confess our sins, he is faithful and just and will forgive us our sins and purify us from all unrighteousness" (1 John 1:9). Guess what "all" means in that verse? All means all. No matter what we've done, God will forgive us and wipe our slates clean. That's a promise.

In no way do I want to diminish the seriousness of sin. Neither do I want to lessen the truth of grace. It was our sin that drove Jesus to the cross. But God's grace is greater than our sin. All sin, always.

The most frequently used words translated *confess*—or *confession*—in the Bible are *yada* in the Old Testament, and *homologeo* in the New Testament. Both mean "to acknowledge." To confess our sin is to acknowledge or agree with God about our sin. Both words also imply repentance and being truly sorry for the sin. Repentance is turning away from the sin and turning toward the Savior. Or, to turn away from what is evil and turn toward what is good.

Remember, when the religious leaders took the woman caught in adultery to Jesus, he did not condemn her. He forgave her. But before she turned to walk away, Jesus said, "Go and sin no more" (John 8:11 NLT). That is the key to true repentance. It is more than being sorry for getting caught. It is a sincere sorrow for having sinned against God. It is a change of the mind that changes behavior.

When we confess our sin, the next step is to believe God tells the truth about removing our sin. God says, "I, even I, am he who blots out your transgressions, for my own sake, and remembers your sins no more" (Isaiah 43:25). Do you believe God tells the truth—that you are completely forgiven and free of accusation? That's the question, isn't it?

The writer of Hebrews said, "Let us run with endurance the race that is set before us, looking to Jesus, the founder and perfecter of our faith, who for the joy that was set before him *endured the cross, despising the shame*, and is seated at the right hand of the throne of God (12:1–2 ESV, emphasis added). Jesus took the shame so we wouldn't have to. When we say that we can't forgive ourselves, it is as if we're saying that what Jesus did was not enough, that there must be something more we have to do.

There is nothing more, no matter what the devil tells you. It's one thing to take personal responsibility for our actions, which I believe we should. It is another to take personal responsibility for our redemption, which we never could.

OUR CHOICE TO LIVE FREE OF SHAME

Can we be saved from sin but still enslaved to shame? Absolutely. Jesus removes the *reason* for shame, but we have to walk out from under the *season* of shame to live free.

Salvation does not instantly inoculate anyone from *feelings* of shame. Forgiving the person who hurt you does not immediately eradicate the *feelings* of shame for what was done to you. Forgiving yourself does not automatically erase the *feelings* of shame over what you've done. But feelings don't always line up with facts. We have to decide to walk away from that shame place, regardless of what our feelings are telling us at the time.

Feelings of shame are rooted in what we tell ourselves about ourselves. Shame keeps us stuck in a loop of condemning thoughts. We can stop the looping lies with the saber of truth. The Bible says, "Therefore, there is now no condemnation for those who are in Christ Jesus" (Romans 8:1). And Paul wrote as well, "Therefore, if anyone is in Christ, the new creation has come: The old has gone, the new is here!" (2 Corinthians 5:17).

The devil sings you the song of shame to keep you from having a better story. To keep you hidden. To keep you quiet. To snuff out your potential. It is a quiet epidemic that sickens God's people. The refusal to forgive ourselves locks us up in the shackles of shame and then hands over the key to the enemy.

Shame isn't a problem only for those who have committed wrongs or experienced personal trauma. It is a part of all of us. Every single person born after the fall will experience shame at one time or another. We may not understand where the feeling comes from, but we all know when something is not quite right. The writer of Romans reminds us, "For all have sinned and fall short of the glory of God" (3:23). And with that falling short comes the weight of shame.

While most think that shame hides in dark corners of life, it actually operates in the open to contaminate areas of everyday life. Even when we think it's hidden, shame operates much as the bitterness of unforgiveness does—it affects our marriages, our parenting, our friendships, our work relationships, and ultimately our decisions. That's why we need to put up a "Do Not Enter" sign and refuse to let shame take up residence in our hearts.

Shame over your failures or your traumas does not define you and does not have to confine you. God can use both to refine you. Your greatest mistakes and your greatest miseries have the potential to become your greatest miracles. Learn the lessons from your suffering, but don't fixate on the failure or the trauma. Receive God's forgiveness and healing and move on.

MOVING THE CORD OF SHAME

Shame had set up house in Rahab's home. Let's look through the peephole of her front door and see how it happened. It all went down, literally, around 1400 BCE.

When it came time for the second generation of Israelites who had been freed from Egyptian slavery to enter the promised land, Joshua sent two spies into Jericho to check out the city. At the time, Jericho had about fifteen hundred to two thousand people living behind the forty-foot-high walls. The gates were tightly shut up for fear of the Israelites, but somehow these two spies slipped in.

When the two men entered the city, they looked for a place to stay and decided on a prostitute's home, which was also her place of business. This may seem like a shocker to us, but not so for them. It was actually an ingenious cover. After all, men traveling through town would often stay at a prostitute's house. And, most likely, it would be the last place the men of Jericho would expect God's people to visit.

How did the spies know she was a prostitute? In certain ancient cities, prostitutes hung a red or scarlet cord on their door. This is what we would call the red-light district today. The scarlet cord meant she was a prostitute open for business—and, no doubt, it was also a sign of her shame. No little girl dreams about growing up to become a prostitute. I can't even imagine the shame Rahab must have felt with the whole town knowing what she did behind that closed door.

The spies were looking for an inconspicuous place to enter and a discreet place from which to depart. Rahab's house in the wall had both. She lived, not *behind* the city walls of Jericho, but actually *within* the five- to seven-foot thickness of the city walls. Her front door opened inward to the city, and her window opened outward to the lands beyond the city walls. Hers was the perfect place to enter and exit.

Shortly after the spies entered her home, someone must have exposed their cover, because the king of Jericho sent word for Rahab to send them out. However, she had hidden them under stalks of flax on her roof and told the king's men they had fled. Rahab then spoke to the men, telling them that all of Jericho had heard of the amazing things the Lord had done for them. She also made a request. Let's listen in on the conversation.

"Now then, please swear to me by the LORD that you will show kindness to my family, because I have shown kindness to you. Give me a sure sign that you will spare the lives of my father and mother, my brothers and sisters, and all who belong to them—and that you will save us from death."

"Our lives for your lives!" the men assured her. "If you don't tell what we are doing, we will treat you kindly and faithfully when the LORD gives us the land."

So she let them down by a rope through the window, for the house she lived in was part of the city wall. She said to them, "Go to the hills so the pursuers will not find you. Hide yourselves there three days until they return, and then go on your way."

Now the men had said to her, "This oath you made us swear will not be binding on us unless, when we enter the land, you have tied this scarlet cord in the window through which you let us down, and unless you have brought your father and mother, your brothers and all your family into your house. . . ."

"Agreed," she replied. "Let it be as you say."

So she sent them away, and they departed. And she tied the scarlet cord in the window. (Joshua 2:12–21)

I'm jumping up and down right now, and it's really hard to type when you're having a praise-party moment. Let's connect the dots. What was the sign of Rahab's greatest shame? The scarlet cord hanging from her door. What was the sign of her glorious salvation to come? The same scarlet cord hanging from her window. Do you see it? The spies didn't carry a scarlet cord around with them; they used hers.

I imagine every time a man walked out of Rahab's door, he took a little piece of her with him. Shame, shame, shame. Weighty shame. But then came the spies—men who knew Yahweh firsthand. Rahab had heard about the God who parted seas, brought manna from the sky, and poured water from a rock, but she had never before met any-one who had seen the miracles with his own eyes. I marvel at her faith. She believed in Yahweh from the mere whispers of his name, and she wanted to know him more.

I expect Rahab moved the scarlet cord from the door to the win-dow that very night. She was no longer open for business, but open to God's perfect plan of rescue, restoration, and redemption.

We don't know how long Rahab waited for the spies to return; I bet it felt like a lifetime. But then one day she heard the rumble of sol-diers' feet circling the city. The ground shook and the walls trembled. For six days, the unnerving processional set the inhabitants of the city on edge. And Rahab waited.

Would the spies keep their promise? Would they even remember to look for the scarlet cord? On the seventh day, she found out. The army marched around the walls seven times and then let out a battle cry such as she had never heard before. Her house within the walls shook. The ceiling began to crumble and fall at her feet, the stones tumbled in a heap. Cries rang out from the people inside the collapsing fortification. Then, her anxious eyes spotted a soldier pointing to the scarlet cord, and her new life began.

The sign of her shame became the sign of her salvation. The sign of her worst chapter became the symbol of her greatest victory! That's what this book is all about—moving the cord from the door you're hiding behind to the open window for all to see. We don't need to hide behind the door of shame for one more minute. The window of grace is open, and all we have to do to escape is climb out. David wrote, "Those who look to him are radiant; their faces are never covered with shame" (Psalm 34:5).

Even wearing a cross around our necks shows how Jesus' worst chapter became his greatest victory—and ultimately ours. In ancient times, the cross was an instrument of torture and death, the ulti-mate sign of shame and condemnation. Because of Jesus' death and resurrection, the cross has become for us not a symbol of shame, but a symbol of victory (Hebrews 12:2).

God's promise to me and you is the same as the promise the spies made to Rahab—he will treat us kindly and faithfully. *Give me that cord,* God says. *Stop hiding behind the door in shame and escape through the window of your salvation. I want that symbol of your shame—that abortion, that affair, that sexual molestation, that parental abuse, that drug addiction, that scarlet cord—I want that. Give that to me and I'll make it a sign of redemption so others can hear about what a miraculous transformation, magnificent restoration, and marvelous inspiration you are today. That thing that was your greatest shame will be your greatest victory. Your worst chapter will become your greatest story.*

When the spies showed up at Rahab's door, she chose to believe that her life could be different. Are you willing to believe that your life could be different? God never means for us to stay stuck in our shame place. The devil means for us to stay there forever.

The spies found the scarlet cord hanging from Rahab's window and saved her and her entire family (Joshua 6:22–25). What became of her after that? She married an Israelite man named Salmon, had a son named Boaz, who had a son named Obed, who had a son name Jesse, who had a son named David—King David. Eventually, she was named in the lineage of Jesus. In fact, she was one of only five women included in the lineage of Jesus recorded in Matthew 1, and one of only a handful of women named as examples of great faith in Hebrews 11. In making the list of examples, the writer of Hebrews didn't mention King David but made sure to include David's great-great-grandma, Rahab.

BUSTING THE WALL OF SHAME

Let's go back to my friend Pat, whose story I shared at the beginning of this chapter. After she and Mike separated, they both began seeing other people. She went to a therapist, who encouraged her to end the marriage. "It's just not working," she said. "You need to end it."

But something in Pat's heart didn't feel that was the best advice. One day while driving home from work, she noticed a counseling center with a welcoming sign. She decided to turn in to the parking lot and ended up making an appointment with a counselor named Carol. What Pat didn't know was that Carol was a Christian with an entirely different belief system from the previous counselor.

Pat told Carol everything, including the story of her abortion. She knew that the abortion was a link to her unhappiness but couldn't put her finger on why. After asking some tender questions, the counselor said, "You have walked away from the Lord and you will not get well until you turn your life back to him. Can I pray for you?" Pat wasn't even sure what that meant, but she agreed. After she left the office, Pat felt like a different person even though she couldn't explain the reason for the change. She drove by Mike's apartment and asked him to come home. He did.

A relationship with Jesus was a foreign concept to Pat, but she decided to attend her neighborhood church. Mike opted to stay home. She dropped off her two sons at Sunday school and sat on the back pew. A beautiful young mom, Terri, walked over and welcomed Pat to church. Sunday worship became her pattern for the next few months, and every Sunday Terri made it a point to sit by Pat.

One day, Terri handed Pat a flyer with information about a women's retreat. "I'd like you to come as my guest," she smiled. "We can room together. It'll be fun."

Even though she had no idea what happened at a women's retreat, Pat agreed to go. The first night, the speaker explained the gospel message of salvation and Pat committed her life to Christ! Afterward, she joined a Bible study and immersed herself in learning more about having a relationship with Jesus. A few months later, both of her boys made decisions to follow Christ. Then, on Christmas Eve, Mike decided to attend church with the family, and he gave his life to Christ as well. In a six-month period, the entire family experienced new life in Christ.

But what about that abortion? Unfortunately, neither Pat nor Mike ever mentioned it. It remained a secret swept under the rug, and they continued to trip over that secret every time they walked through the door of their home. In her book *Rising Strong*, Brené Brown wrote:

> When we deny our stories and disengage from tough emotions, they don't go away; instead, they own us, they define us. Our job is not to deny the story, but to defy the ending—to rise strong, recognize our story, and rumble with the truth until we get to a place where we think, *Yes. This is what happened. This is my truth. And I will choose how this story ends.*[5]

A low rumble in the distance was headed straight toward Pat's heart.

Six months after Pat became a Christ follower, she was listening to her local Christian radio station and heard two women talking about how God had healed them from the shame of past abortions. Pat wasn't even sure God knew about her abortion, and she certainly couldn't imagine telling her new Christian friends about it. The interview unnerved her, and she turned off the radio. The secret she'd tried so hard to hide was slowly rising to the surface.

The next week, Pat went to a Christian bookstore to purchase a book that would help her "fix" her husband. And what should greet her at the door? A display showcasing a book by a woman who had an abortion while in seminary. *This can't be happening*, Pat thought to herself. She bought the book and devoured it in a day. Pat knew that God was telling her it was time to share her story. The Christian counselor she had previously seen walked Pat through the steps of healing from post-traumatic stress syndrome as it related to abortion.

Then she took Mike through the steps as well. God had a plan. He always does. The promise of Romans 8:28, that God was working all things together for good, swirled around them.

But Pat worried that if she told her story, she would face rejection, condemnation, and isolation. After all, people saw her as a well-put-together, successful, morally upright part of the community. Her new friends liked her. What would they think of her if they knew the truth? But Pat didn't let fear of rejection stop her. And she knew that the first person she wanted to tell was Terri, the one person who had earned the right to hear her story.

Through a flood of tears, Pat told Terri she needed to tell her a secret that she had hidden for a long time. Terri put her arms around her trembling friend and assured her, "There's nothing you can't tell me. I love you no matter what."

So she told her story, leaving no painful detail undisclosed. She was amazed at the love and compassion she saw in Terri's eyes. This was not what she expected. Then Terri placed her hand on Pat's and assured her, "I've never had an abortion, but I have made other bad choices in my life. My college days are filled with regrets. God doesn't measure one sin as worse than another. Sin is sin. I think you need to tell this story to Pastor Brooks."

Courage grows when we act courageously. The second time Pat told her story, she had just a smidgen more. The gentle older man listened compassionately as Pat spoke. When she finished, he held both her hands in his and said, "Pat, God has a calling on your life. He has called you to make a difference in this area of abortion. Revelations 12:11 says, 'And they overcame him,' meaning the devil, 'by the blood of the Lamb and by the word of their testimony.' You have a powerful testimony. I believe God has called you for such a time as this to make a difference in the world."[6]

A few months later, Pat and her husband looked for centers that helped women in crisis pregnancy situations so that they could volunteer. When they found none in their area, they sensed God nudging them to start one. Where? In the very building Pat had leased for her insurance business. With great anticipation and joy, Pat took a sledgehammer and busted down a wall to expand the space. With each swing, another layer of shame fell from her heart. Her tears mingled with the cheers from those who watched. All those years of pent-up shame and regret released like a flood bursting through a broken dam. The scarlet cord of shame became the scarlet cord of redemption. What Pat once considered the worst part of her story, God is now using for his best—the saving of many lives.

Courage grows when we act courageously.

Chapter Seven

When Forgetting Is Not Enough

*The closest communion with God comes, I
believe, through the sacrament of tears. Just as
grapes are crushed to make wine and grain to
make bread, so the elements of this sacrament
come from the crushing experiences of life.*

—Ken Gire, *Windows of the Soul*

Aaron was Gail's only son, the older brother to two adoring sisters. Growing up an athletic middle child with two sisters herself, Gail had always wanted a son. From the moment Aaron made his first cry, he and his mom had a special bond. When he went away to college 570 miles from home, part of Gail's heart went with him. Her greatest fear was that something would happen to one of her three children.

One hot summer day in June, Aaron's friend Tyler invited him to go rafting down the James River in their college town of Lynchburg, Virginia. The James was swollen due to heavy rains, and it promised to be an exhilarating ride. They each had their own small raft but vowed to stay close together. Tyler held on tight as he maneuvered the rapids and made it to calm waters. Then he stopped to watch Aaron do the same. Aaron also held on tight, but his raft flipped over and he went under. Tyler waited for Aaron to resurface from the angry waters, but he never did.

The next four days were the worst story Gail could ever have imagined. She and several family members drove from Rhode Island to Lynchburg. She held Aaron's picture to her chest and kept repeating a promise from the psalms: "'Because he loves me,' says the LORD, 'I will rescue him; I will protect him, for he acknowledges my name'" (Psalm 91:14).

When they arrived at the spot on the river where the boats had flipped, rescue workers surrounded them. Search dogs barked. Low-flying helicopters whirled. Police officers marked off the area with yellow tape. A CSI crew with block letters on their black jackets scoured the scene. But even in the midst of all this, Gail felt an indescribable and undeniable peace.

The dogs picked up Aaron's scent along the bank, but that was all . . . just the scent. After four days, the rescue workers made the tough decision to call off the search. "We may never find his body," one said. "He may have been swept out to the bay."

"But this is my baby!" Gail cried. "You've got to find him! I will not go home without him!"

Gail thought of the words she'd seen in Aaron's devotion book that still lay on his nightstand. The pages were open to June 30, the day of the accident: "He lifted me out of the slimy pit, out of the mud and mire" (Psalm 40:2).

As Gail drove from her hotel back to Aaron's apartment the next morning, a song played on the car radio. "Go rest high on that mountain," Vince Gill sang. "Son, your work on earth is done." Stunned, Gail looked at the clock. It read 11:30.

Moments later, a rescue worker called and asked Gail and her family to meet them at the fire station. When the ambulance turned the corner and came into view, she knew.

One of the men knelt down in front of Gail. "Gail," he began with tears in his eyes and a comforting soft smile on his face, "we found your boy."

"Can I see him?" she asked.

"No, Gail, you can't."

"What time did you find him?" she asked with trembling lips.

"Eleven thirty a.m.," he replied.

And Gail remembered the song.

When I first met Gail, I was struck by her bubbly personality and effervescent joy. Her dancing blue eyes. Her wide, inviting smile. Her ready laugh. She's the kind of person you just want to be around in hopes that whatever she's got will rub off on you. When she told me her story, I struggled to reconcile the peace I saw on her face and the worst possible chapter any parent could experience. I thought of my own son, born the same year as Gail's.

But Aaron's homegoing wasn't the end of her story; it was only the beginning. Gail told me account after account of how God had used her story to help others going through similar experiences. She is a living example of how our worst chapters can become our greatest victories, but she didn't start out that way.

After Aaron's funeral, Gail went to bed and thought she'd never get up. Just a few months earlier, when discussing a New Year's weekend trip to New York, Aaron had told her, "Mom, if anything ever happens to me, I will go to heaven. I'll be fine."

"Son, if something happened to you, and you went to heaven, you might as well take me with you," she said. "I wouldn't be able to live after that."

Gail wasn't kidding. She meant it. "God," she cried, "I've prayed for Aaron his entire life, and this is what I get?" Confused. Angry. Lost. Empty. Impotent. And even though she still had a loving husband and two adoring daughters, Gail couldn't get up the energy it took to live. She lost vision for her future, because she had no hope that life could be different than it was at that moment. She stopped going to church and her Bible stayed shut.

Three months later, Gail's daughter, Jacqueline, asked her to attend a Beth Moore conference with her. "Oh, heck no," was Gail's quick reply.

"Mom, you need to go. I need to go. We need this."

So, Gail agreed to go along. She told Jacqueline and God, "I'll go, but I'm not going to listen."

At the conference, after the lunch break, the usually perky Beth came out on stage looking solemn. "I was on my knees praying during the break," Beth began, "and God put it on my heart that there is a woman here that lost her son this summer. I want to tell you, it's okay to be angry."

Gail doesn't remember the rest of what Beth said, because her mind began to spin. She knew that God had stopped for her. Loved her. Remembered her. And at that very moment, God was wooing her back. She was going to be okay.

"Yes, I grieved," Gail shared. "Even though I saw God's fingerprints throughout the entire ordeal, even though I sensed his presence surrounding our family and friends, I was still mad at him. But God stayed right there with me. He didn't give up on me, but lovingly wooed me, pursued me, and loved me back to life. He pulled *me* from the muck and mire. Healing has been a process. Eventually, I knew I had to let go and take hold of the promises of God as never before. I still miss Aaron. What gets me through is the knowledge that I will see Aaron again. Perhaps one of the biggest steps in the healing process was when I turned around and used my story to help someone who was going through a similar situation."

HEALING IS A PROCESS

As we've seen in the last couple of chapters, forgiveness begins with a decision; so, too, does walking out from under the shadow of the shame place. But healing is a process. Whether we're talking about Pat's healing from the results of a decision she wishes she could take back, my healing of violent childhood memories, or Gail's healing from the death of her son, healing takes time.

Healing begins by recognizing that a broken heart needs mending, a busted life needs repairing, the consequences of a regrettable decision need righting. It starts with a decision to "get well"—to set the shattered bone of contention, to lance the festering boil of bitterness, to remove the rotting soul ache of resentment, to stop metastatic memories from spreading. God cannot heal what we do not reveal, and the process requires words. Healing peeks through the birth canal of wholeness when we tell someone our story for the first time.

Because healing is a process, it doesn't usually happen in an instant, but through a series of steps or decisions. It's not a sprint, but a marathon—one with potholes, bends in the road, and a few straightaways that build momentum. A process implies movement—a progression from one step to the next. I hope you've seen that as we've moved through these pages together.

Honestly, I'm not a fan of process. I prefer instant. One of my favorite words in the New Testament is *immediately*.

"Immediately they received their sight" (Matthew 20:34).

"Immediately the leprosy left him" (Mark 1:42).

"Immediately her bleeding stopped" (Luke 8:44).

Sometimes, God does heal *immediately*. But that's not always how God works. Most times, he heals us through a progression of healing steps.

I grew up with a world of wounds from what went on in my home. I couldn't wait to graduate from high school and get out of that house. The problem was, when I left, I took my memories with me. I was a Christian, I loved Jesus, but I was weighed down with anger and resentment for what my parents had done and what they had not done. My healing came over time in layers of forgiveness, stages of shedding shame, and progressively learning to see myself as God saw me. Just when I thought I was in the clear, God would reveal another closet of my heart that needed cleaning out.

When we have a physical wound, the need for attention is obvious. We sew up the cut, bind the break, bandage the burn. Then we douse the injury with medicine and wait for it to heal. Once a scar has formed or the bone has set, we know the body has repaired itself. The area may still be tender for a while, and it might take some time before we stop being mindful of it, but the wound is closed, and a healthy scar remains.

But when we are wounded emotionally, it's not quite that straightforward. We can't see the wound, so it often goes unattended, festering and spreading infection into our thoughts and relationships. Time does not heal all wounds, especially wounds of the heart. They may lie dormant for a season, but triggers poke them with the hot iron of remembrance that lets us know they're still there.

We've talked about making a decision to forgive, but there is also a process that follows even that decision. The mind and the emotions don't always move in tandem. Emotions tend to lag behind. Even when we make a sincere decision to forgive, it might take a while for our emotions to catch up.

Emotional triggers are like switches that flip the light on hurtful memories and make us feel them all over again. They can bring back the hurt and make us think we've never forgiven in the first place. When that happens, rather than listening to the lies that tell you that you never forgave, speak to your soul and remind yourself that you already have.

MOVING BEYOND ACCEPTANCE

Sometimes healing requires grieving. Grief is a natural response to a loss. It could be the loss of a loved one, the loss of a relationship, or the loss of a dream. Grief is a complex weaving of emotions that accompany the loss of what was or sometimes the emptiness of what wasn't.

In her classic book *On Death and Dying*, Elisabeth Kubler-Ross noted five stages of grief:[1]

- Stage One: Denial and Isolation
- Stage Two: Anger
- Stage Three: Bargaining
- Stage Four: Depression
- Stage Five: Acceptance

But for us who know Jesus Christ, there is a sixth stage:

- Resurrection

Oh, sweet friend, Jesus died on that cross, but then he rose again. He left his grave so that you could leave yours. Your dreams of what you had hoped your story would be may have died on the cross of unmet expectations or unwanted violation, but your dreams can rise again. They may even become someone else's inspiration to rise up from their grave of broken dreams as well.

I grieved that I did not grow up being the apple of my daddy's eye. My friend Angela grieved the loss of investing in a thirty-five-year marriage that ended in divorce. Gail grieved the loss of her son in the chilling waters of the James River. Pat grieved the loss of her unborn child by her own decision. Grieving is part of the healing process.

Each of the women I just named mourned her losses but eventually moved on to write new chapters of her story. After a time, we all stopped lamenting what was not and started looking for the blessing of what is. That doesn't mean we don't miss the child or lament the loss, but we don't get stuck there. It doesn't mean that we don't hurt any longer, but the wound no longer controls our decisions or actions.

We've stopped slapping away God's hand from the pen and look forward to seeing how he will write the rest of the storyline. Sometimes our healing process includes counselors or therapists, sometimes it includes medication to get us through the worst of it, but it always includes the healing of Jesus Christ and our cooperation with the Holy Spirit to get back up.

Perhaps you need to grieve for losses in your life. Here are a few:

- Loss of innocence
- Loss of a marriage
- Loss of a relationship with your mother
- Loss of a relationship with your father
- Loss of employment
- Loss of a spouse
- Loss of a child
- Loss of friendship
- Loss of hopes and dreams

In the Bible, the prophet Samuel grieved the loss of what could have been had King Saul obeyed rather than ignored God. He literally went to bed and pulled the covers up over his sad head. But after a while, God told him it was time to get back up and keep moving forward. God had the pen in his hand and was ready to write the next chapters. God said to Samuel, "How long will you mourn for Saul, since I have rejected him as king over Israel? Fill your horn with oil and be on your way; I am sending you to Jesse of Bethlehem. I have chosen one of his sons to be king" (1 Samuel 16:1).

It was time for Samuel to get out of bed and for God's resurrection plan to move forward. God had chosen a new king. His name was David.

THE BETTER BLESSING

Joseph was the boy with a coat of many colors who became a man of many talents who we met in chapter 3. After he confronted and forgave his brothers for selling him into what seemed like a series of tragic events, Pharaoh invited Joseph's entire extended family to come live in Egypt. They settled in Goshen, east of the Nile, which featured some of the best grazing land available. In grace upon grace, even though the famine still ravaged the land, they never knew a day of hunger.

Meanwhile, Joseph stayed near the palace. During his years in Egypt, Joseph and his wife, Asenath, had two sons. He named his firstborn Manasseh, which means "God has made me forget completely my hardship and my parental home."[2] The second son he named Ephraim, which means "God has made me fruitful or fertile in the land of my affliction."[3]

One day, Joseph learned that his father was dying, so he took his two sons, Manasseh and Ephraim, to see their grandfather one last time. When they arrived, Jacob asked Joseph to bring the boys to his bedside so he could bless them.

Jacob's eyes were weak with age, and he could barely see. So, Joseph led the boys to his father's bedside. He placed Ephraim in front of Jacob's left hand and Manasseh, his firstborn, in front of Jacob's right hand—the hand that would give blessing. But then Jacob did something that startled them all. He reached out his right hand and placed it on the head of second-born Ephraim, and crossed his arm over to place his left hand on the head of firstborn Manasseh.

"No, Dad," Joseph said, "you've got it all wrong. Your right hand goes on Manasseh's head and your left hand goes on Ephraim's."

But Jacob knew exactly what he was doing. While Manasseh would become a people in his own right, his younger brother's people would be greater (Genesis 48:19).

Okay, interesting story, except for poor Manasseh. But this is why I love the Bible. It is so rich with meaning. Hold on to your hat.

Where does the true blessing come? Where does the full circle of healing occur? Not just when we forget our suffering (Manasseh), but when we become fruitful in our suffering (Ephraim). Yes, Joseph had a tumultuous life filled with family strife, false accusation, and brotherly betrayal, but God didn't want him to merely forget about it. God wanted him to be fruitful in it, to come full circle and bless the very ones who had hurt him. And that's why we're still telling his story today.

And it's the same for you and me. God doesn't want us to simply forget our suffering. Healing does not mean forgetting. He wants us to be fruitful in our suffering. Suffering can become seed in our hands. We can choose to slip those seeds in little packets and store them away, or we can choose to sprinkle those seeds as good news of how God brought us through in the well-tilled soil of a ready soul. That's what it means to be fruitful. That's when healing happens. That's when we cross over from bitter to better once and for all—when our stories give hope to others that life can be different on the other side of pain. Your heartache can become someone else's hope.

A Christian's final phase of grief, *resurrection*, takes us back once again to God's promise of good: "And we know that in all things God works for the good of those who love him, who have been called according to his purpose" (Romans 8:28). Perhaps the most important part of "works for the good" is the leap from acceptance to resurrection by telling someone your story and giving them hope. Again, *the pages we would most likely want to remove from our story, God wants to repurpose for his glory.* When being fruitful in our suffering overrides forgetting our suffering, healing comes full circle and brings glory to God. That's what Gail experienced after her son Aaron's homegoing.

COME SIT WITH ME

God continued to write new chapters for Gail and her family. Six years after Aaron drowned in the James River, a woman in Gail's church lost her son to suicide. Like Gail, Kim went through all the stages of grief. One place she refused to return to was church. Even the thought of walking through those doors opened up a flood of tears. Her son, Todd, had been a joy to raise, but after high school he made an avalanche of bad choices that left him in a deep depression. On a cold December night, with a stolen gun, Todd ended his pain. But for his mom and the rest of the family, Todd's suicide was just the beginning of a kind of pain they could never have imagined. Kim had been there for his boo-boos, poison ivy, and broken bones, but she could not save him from this.

Kim tried many different avenues to alleviate her suffering, but the paralyzing pain lingered. After two and a half years, she took a deep breath and walked back through the doors of the church she had left behind. Kim found her seat near the back, hoping no one would notice. But Gail noticed. Gail invited Kim to sit with her. The two wounded mamas held each other and wept. Every Sunday after that, Kim and Gail were seatmates.

When I asked Kim how Gail had helped her, she said, "The gift of her presence was the greatest gift of all. I didn't want to be open and honest with people because they just didn't understand. God gave me a gift when he gave me Gail. She had lived it. She got it. She could say things to me that no one had earned the right to say. Gail comforted me with *the same comfort* she had received from God, just like it says in the Bible. Even before tragedy struck our family, I watched Gail go through her darkest chapter. I paid attention. I saw how she leaned into the Lord and continued to speak about the goodness of God. And when I was ready, she took my hand and helped me do the same."

Yes, we balk at the bumps and bruises of life, we shrink back at the shattering of the heart, but when we take a step to use what we've gone through to help someone else, I believe healing comes full circle. Resurrection power transforms our stories into beacons of hope.

BECOMING A HOPE GIVER

"It's going to be okay." That is one of the most hope-filled sentiments I can offer to others, and that I choose to believe for myself. I love how French philosopher Gabriel Marcel defined hope as "a memory of the future." In those simple words, he linked that past to the future with the mysterious thread of hope. The writer of Hebrews did the same: "Now faith is being sure of what we hope for, being convinced of what we do not see" (Hebrews 11:1 NET). Of course, for the Christian there is the future hope of eternity with God. But there is also hope for the here and now. We have the assurance, the evidence of things not seen, that no matter what happens, God is still on his throne. Author Dan Allender wrote, "Hope is not the absence of sorrow but a refusal to allow powerlessness to silence our cry or shake our confidence in God."[4]

Unless I know someone has struggled through traumatic situations themselves, I don't really believe them when they tell me, "It's going to be okay." My knee-jerk reaction is, "How do you know?" Unless they truly do understand, the words fall flat. When you aren't ashamed to tell your darkest moments but freely reveal how God brought you through, you become believable. Hope becomes conceivable.

What is biblical hope? It is tethering what we know about God's past faithfulness to the future. In defining faith as "being sure of what we hope for," the writer of Hebrews gives us an insight into hope, but let's chew on it a bit. Biblical hope is not a wish. A wish is something we want to have or to happen. "I wish I had a house." "I wish I could go to Spain." "I wish I had a smaller waist." Maybe it will happen one day, maybe it won't. In contrast, biblical hope is a certainty that our ultimate future rests in God's capable and loving hands. It is an assurance that the invisible God is faithful and has a good plan in my visible life.

Old Testament writers used several Hebrew words for *hope*. One is *qawa*, which means hope in the sense of trust, as when the prophet Jeremiah said to God, "Our hope is in you" (Jeremiah 14:22).[5] New Testament writers used the Greek word *hupomeno*, which means to wait, to be patient, to endure, to persevere under misfortunes and trials to hold fast to one's faith in Christ. It is only through a sense of *qawa* trust in God that we can experience the *hupomeno* type of hope that Paul had. Paul encountered struggle after struggle, but he never lost hope that everything was going to be okay. In The Message, Eugene Peterson captured Paul's hopeful outlook this way:

> So we're not giving up. How could we! Even though on the outside it often looks like things are falling apart on us, on the inside, where God is making new life, not a day goes by without his unfolding grace. These hard times are small potatoes compared to the coming good times, the lavish celebration prepared for us. There's far more here than meets the eye. The things we see now are here today, gone tomorrow. But the things we can't see now will last forever. (2 Corinthians 4:16–18 THE MESSAGE)

How can your worst chapters become your greatest victories? One way is to use the ways God has healed you to give hope to others—to show someone that you've traversed the same or similar rocky soil and made it to level ground.

Theologian Rubem Alves once said, "Hope is hearing the melody of the future. Faith is to dance to it."[6] One of the ways we can dance to it—and take another step toward complete healing—is to take the hand of a sojourner who has lost hope and share our melody.

Sometimes, it may take years to put back the pieces the wrecking ball of pain has caused. The atrocities we've endured may tempt us to believe that someone other than God is writing our stories. But I trust you've caught a glimpse of what God can do with even the most shattered of stories. He has the power to redeem what we consider unredeemable. To heal what we consider fatally wounded. To make our worst chapters our greatest victories. And then to fashion us into hope-givers who are believable, vulnerable, and beautiful.

When tragedy tears our hearts out, when untimely death cracks the foundation of our faith, when abuse mars all that is good, we mourn. We grieve the loss. But we mustn't allow the story to stop there. I type these words with tears in my eyes because I have lived them. Hear me when I say, it's going to be okay—you're going to be okay. God has more to write. Resurrection is on the way.

Chapter Eight

Why Your Story Matters

Come and listen, all you who fear God,
and I will tell you what he did for me.

—Psalm 66:16 NLT

Poor Daddy. He just couldn't shake it. Shame weighed him down like a dead body strapped to his back. No matter how many times I told him that God loved and accepted him just the way he was, he couldn't believe it. That kind of grace was unfathomable, unthinkable, unbelievable . . . especially for a man like him.

How does a body get so low he feels there's no getting out of the hole he's dug? How does a soul see beyond the wrong done to him and through him? How does a pierced heart heal when the knife still turns in tender flesh?

I've shared how the home I grew up in was rife with angry outbursts, violent arguments, alcohol-induced mayhem. My dad was an emotionally active volcano with occasional periods of dormancy. My mom was a bitter and wounded woman who sometimes had stretches of sweet normalcy. I was just scared.

But God didn't leave us that way. Don't you just love the words "But God"? They are two of my favorite words in the entire Bible. It is often with that one little word *but* that God's plot takes an unexpected turn.

When I was twelve years old, my best friend was Wanda Henderson. We'd snuggle down in thick comforters when I spent the night at her house and tell little-girl secrets. Those secrets eventually made it around to me telling her what was going on at my house. And later, she coaxed me to tell her mom.

Mrs. Henderson took me under her wing. She told me about Jesus who loved me and a heavenly Father who adored me. She not only explained the gospel to me, she lived it for me to see. I spent many Saturday nights at the Hendersons' home and went to church with them the following day.

Amazingly, my family, as bad as we were, also went to church on Sundays. We'd walk in the pristine doors and people would say, "How are you today?" "Fine, just fine," we'd reply. We were anything but fine. We were just good Americans doing what Southern families did back then.

But the Hendersons' church was different. What I know now is that my family had a religion; the Henderson family had a relationship with Jesus. I didn't understand the difference at the time. All I knew was that I wanted what they had.

For two years, Mrs. Henderson mentored me without even knowing it. She was just going about life being her joyful, Jesus-lovin' self, but I watched her every move. She sang praise songs when she did her housework, called her gregarious husband pet names, and talked to and about Jesus as if he were her best friend. One night, when I was fourteen, she sat me down on the den sofa, took my hands in hers, and asked, "Sharon, would you like to ask Jesus to be your Lord and Savior? Would you like to become a Christian?"

I said yes.

Mrs. Henderson prayed. I cried. We all rejoiced.

But the next day, I had to go back home. Tension still ran high, and nothing much changed, except that my friends and I began to pray for my messed-up family.

Three years later, when I was seventeen, I had an opportunity to go away for the summer to study with a group of foreign exchange students. "How can I go?" I told my friends. "I can't leave my parents!" By this time, I was the one who broke up the fights between my parents. Like a referee ringing the bell, I'd jump between them and pull them apart. Who would do that if I weren't there?

But I also sensed God asking, *Will you trust me?*

So I decided to go.

The night before I left, I told my mom, "I'm not going to be here to help you. If something happens, go down to Mrs. Henderson's house. She'll help you."

And off I went. That first night I was away, my dad came home drunk and started a fight, which led to my mom running down to the Hendersons. And that night, after three years of God's great pursuit, my mom gave her life to Christ.

She went back home and told Dad that she forgave him for everything he had ever done and that she was going to love him no matter what. From that moment on, my dad never drank again. Now, hear me on this—I would never tell a woman being abused to stay with her husband and allow that behavior to continue. She needs to be safe, and staying in an abusive situation is not safe. If that is you, get help right away. Don't hide in the shame of it all. You are not alone.

When I came home at the end of the summer, I heard all the details. My teary-eyed dad told me, "Sharon, I'll go to church with you and your mom, but I've done too many terrible things in my life to ever become a Christian. God could never forgive me." Of course, I explained that none of us could ever be good enough. If we could, then Jesus wouldn't have had to die for our sins. All we have to do is ask for forgiveness and he wipes the slate clean. But Dad couldn't understand that kind of grace.

And even though my dad agreed to go to church with us, he never believed that God could forgive a man like him.

A MAN LIKE HIM

Dad had many vices. Alcohol, pornography, gambling, and illicit relationships with other women—all common knowledge in the small town where we lived. And while the drinking stopped and the physical violence stopped, some of his other vices continued.

My father had always been a successful businessman, but during my twentieth year, he began to experience a maze of twists and turns that only God could have orchestrated. He resigned from the company where he served as manager to begin his own building-supply business with four other investors. However, his previous employer threatened to sue him because of a restrictive noncompete clause in his prior contract. He was facing a court battle, exposure for God only knew what, and ruination in our small town. Buckling under the pressure, Dad was heading toward a nervous breakdown. But God dipped his pen in the inkwell and continued writing one of his best stories ever.

One day, Dad drove home in a panic, only to remember that my mom was at an arts-and-crafts supply show in Pennsylvania. She owned a shop called the Bee 'N' Beetle and was at a wholesaler's event. Dad hopped in his car and drove the four hundred miles from North Carolina to Pennsylvania to try and find her. Once there, he stopped by a random church.

"Is the preacher here?" he pled. "I need someone to pray for me!"

"I'm sorry," the receptionist replied. "He's not in at the moment. But I know that Clyde Barnes, the pastor of the church down the street, is out doing some construction on his new church building in the woods." The receptionist grabbed a scrap piece of paper and drew a map. "Why don't you drive on over and find him? I bet he can help."

Dad jumped back in his car and drove to a church out in the country where he found a man with a hammer in his hand and Jesus in his heart.

"I need you to pray for me," Dad explained with tears running down his weathered cheeks.

"Let's sit down here on this log. Now, tell me what's going on," the pastor said.

For several hours, Dad sat with a fellow builder and told him all he had ever done. When my dad finished his confession, the pastor placed his strong arm around my dad's shaking shoulders and said, "Now, Allan, let me tell you what I've done."

"You see, Allan," he began, "I was a man much like you."

The pastor pulled back the curtain on his own dark past and followed with the subsequent unfolding of forgiveness, redemption, and healing from Jesus.

That day, my dad and a pastor whom I'll never know knelt in the woods of Pennsylvania and prayed the sinner's prayer. My dad entered the woods as a sinner and came out a saint.

What turned him around? Well, for sure and for certain it was the power of the Holy Spirit that quickened his dead spirit to life. But there was something more. Because this pastor wasn't ashamed of his story—he wasn't afraid to tell about his past—Dad saw the healing, forgiving, grace-filled power of Jesus up close and personal. His gaping wounds met the balm of grace through a man who was willing to reveal the most despicable parts of his own story and how God forgave him. Dad had finally met a man just like him.

The way my father explained it to me when he came home was: "That man told me *his* story. He had done everything I had done. And I knew that if God could forgive him and he could be a pastor, then he could forgive me too."

I often wonder what would have happened if the pastor had been too ashamed of his past to tell his story. If he had decided to keep the sordid details to himself. I wonder what would have happened if he had just opened up his Bible, quoted a few verses, said a prayer, and sent my dad on his way. I daresay, my father would not have given his life to Christ that day.

When we are not ashamed of our stories but tell how God redeemed our deepest, darkest, dirtiest places, we give hope to desperate sojourners who feel all alone. Suddenly, Jesus isn't just a man in a book or a face in a painting. He becomes the Healer, the Sustainer, the Redeemer. He becomes real.

Remember how Pastor Brooks encouraged my friend Pat Layton to share her story? He quoted the verse that says, "They triumphed over him [the devil] by the blood of the Lamb and by the *word of their testimony*" (Revelation 12:11, emphasis added). Think about it. Your story of redemption—your testimony—has so much power that it is in the same sentence with "the blood of the Lamb." No wonder the devil wants us to keep our stories buried in shallow graves of bitterness, resentment, and shame. No wonder he taunts us with the lie that others will think less of us, reject us, or ridicule us if they know the truth of our past. He knows that the moment we push back the dirt to reveal what God has done, resurrection power will be released. Chains will fall. Broken hearts will mend. Shame will flee. Bitterness will cease. Souls will be saved. *Your story is a divine weapon that has the power to defeat the devil.* It is living proof of Jesus' redemptive power here on earth.

THE POWER OF STORY

Stories are powerful. They are an essential part of what it means to be human. From the dawn of time, stories allowed humans to connect with each other and give meaning to life. Rather than listening to facts, stories help us put ourselves in the scene and experience the emotions, sights, sounds, and stirrings of other people. A story invites us to become partici- *Your story is a* pants rather than mere spectators.

Stories evoke emotion and make otherwise abstract principles come to life. Isn't that what Jesus did all throughout the Gospels? He told stories. Rather than teach forgiveness prin-

> *Your story is a divine weapon that has the power to defeat the devil.*

ciples, Jesus told a story about a man with two sons. One took his inheritance before his father died and squandered it on wild living. After he lost everything he had, the son came to his senses and returned home to his father. His dad forgave him, gave him a new set of clothes, and hosted a grand celebration. In telling the story, Jesus was essentially saying, "There, that's what forgiveness looks like."

Rather than teach about heaven, Jesus told a story about a landowner who went out early in the morning to hire men to work in his vineyard. He went out again and again at multiple times throughout the day. Even at the eleventh hour, with only a little time left in the workday, he hired a few more stragglers. At day's end, he paid all the workers the same wage, whether they had worked all day or just an hour. Again, Jesus was saying, "There, that's what heaven is like."

Story. Ah, we get it.

And what makes a story even better is when it's a real one. When it's your story. When it's mine.

The story of what God has done in your life makes him real to those who hear it. Some might balk at biblical principles or try to argue with theology, but they can't deny a person's personal experience. Stories capture listeners' attention, draw them into the narrative, and stir emotions. People have a natural curiosity about the dark side or struggles of others. Whether or not the listeners' stories are similar to the teller's is not important. Everyone wants to be better than they are at the moment, whether or not they voice that longing. Hearing about how that happened in someone else's life is magnetic. Pastor Rick Warren put it this way: "Shared stories build a relational bridge that Jesus can walk across from your heart to theirs."[1]

In the church, we use the word *testimony* when someone gives an account of what God has done in their lives. Most of the time folks think of a testimony as a salvation story. However, a testimony could be so much more. Coming to Christ is only the beginning—the first page in many exciting chapters to come. It may be the turning point of someone's story, but it is never meant to be the end. A testimony is *any* recounting of what God has done in a person's life. "Let me tell you about what God did for me at the grocery store." "Let me tell you about what God taught me on my walk today." "Let me tell you how God healed my son." "Let me tell you how God restored my marriage." Testimonies, all.

WHAT HAPPENED TO YOU?

One day, Jesus and his disciples were walking down the street when they came upon a man blind from birth. The disciples asked, "Rabbi, who sinned: this man or his parents, causing him to be born blind?" Here's how Eugene Peterson told the story in *The Message:*

> Jesus said, "You're asking the wrong question. You're looking for someone to blame. There is no such cause-effect here. Look instead for what God can do. We need to be energetically at work for the One who sent me here, working while the sun shines. When night falls, the workday is over. For as long as I am in the world, there is plenty of light. I am the world's Light."
>
> He said this and then spit in the dust, made a clay paste with

the saliva, rubbed the paste on the blind man's eyes, and said, "Go, wash at the Pool of Siloam" (Siloam means "Sent"). The man went and washed—and saw. (John 9:3–7)

Boom! Healed. Just like that.

In Jesus' day, it was customary for people to spit on the ground when they walked by someone with a deformity or disability. They believed the infirmity was due to a curse and that they could keep the curse away from themselves by spitting on the ground. When Jesus stopped in front of him, the blind man heard the familiar spit sound, but then felt an unfamiliar touch.

After the man went to the pool of Siloam and washed the mud from his eyes, he could see. The NIV puts it succinctly. "So the man went and washed, and came home seeing" (v. 7). It was just that simple.

When the man went back home, the people were confused. "Is this the same man we have seen begging by the road for so many years?" they asked.

"Nah, couldn't be," some argued. "It only looks like him."

"It's me," the man replied. "It's really me!"

"How did your eyes get opened?" they asked.

"I was sitting on the side of the road. A man named Jesus came by. He spit in the dirt, put mud on my eyes, and told me to wash in the pool of Siloam. I did what he said and now I can see!"

As Jesus often did, he healed the man on the Sabbath. This infuriated the Pharisees who taught that no work should be done on the seventh day. They were more concerned with the binding law than the blinded man. So, they brought the man in and asked, "What happened to you?"

"I was sitting on the side of the road. A man named Jesus came by. He spit in the dirt, put mud on my eyes, and told me to wash in the pool of Siloam. I did what he said and now I can see!"

The Pharisees didn't like that answer, so they called in the man's parents.

They asked them, "Is this your son, the one that you say was born blind? So how is it that he now sees?"

His parents said, "We know he is our son, and we know he was born blind. But we don't know how he came to see—haven't a clue about who opened his eyes. Why don't you ask him? He's a grown man and can speak for himself." . . .

They called the man back a second time . . . and told him, "Give credit to God. We know this man is an impostor."

He replied, "I know nothing about that one way or the other. But I know one thing for sure: I was blind . . . I now see." (vv. 19–21, 24–25 THE MESSAGE)

The man didn't know the Scriptures like the Pharisees did. He couldn't argue the law like the Sadducees could. What he did know was this: "I was sitting on the side of the road. A man named Jesus came by. He spit in the dirt, put mud on my eyes, and told me to wash in the pool of Siloam. I did what he said and now I can see!"

I've paraphrased the account a bit. But here's the point: you just can't refute someone's personal story.

It wasn't the dirt that made the difference in the man's life. It never is. It's what Jesus did with the dirt that was the real miracle. And it's the same with you and me. It's not the dirt of our story that will make a difference in someone else's life. It's what God did with the dirt that is the real miracle. Sharing our dirt makes us relatable; sharing what God did with the dirt makes him visible.

Yes, the formerly blind man now had a story to tell. God planned it all along. Before the miracle took place, Jesus' disciples asked, "'Rabbi, who sinned, this man or his parents, that he was born blind?' 'Neither this man nor his parents sinned,' said Jesus, 'but this happened so that the works of God might be displayed in him" (vv. 2–3). And it was.

What was true in the life of the man born blind is also true in ours. When Jesus heals our hurt, binds our brokenness, and miraculously redeems our messiness, the work of God is displayed in our lives. It's up to us to tell about it.

It's interesting that Jesus told the man to wash in the pool of Siloam. "Siloam" means "sent," and that's exactly what happened to the man after he was healed. He was *sent* to tell others about what God had done in his life.

Every Christian has a story to tell. Maybe you didn't have a meth lab in your basement or work the streets as a prostitute. Perhaps you were raised in a Christian home with loving parents who cherished you. Either way, you were blind, but now you see. You were spiritually dead, and now you are spiritually alive in Christ. Death to life never gets old.

We should never diminish the power of our stories, no matter how dark or disappointing they may be, no matter how boring or uneventful they may seem. Don't hide your story in hopes no one will ever see it. Tell it. Show it. Celebrate God's work through it. Let your story be evidence of your strength and bravery that shouts to the world that a new ending is possible. Realize that your disappointments, bad decisions, and darkest struggles can be the most life-changing parts of your story. Your worst chapters can become your greatest victories.

PUTTING TO USE WHAT GOD BROUGHT YOU THROUGH

Author Levi Lusko called it the Christmas from hell. He loved Christmas, at least he did before this particular Christmas unexpectedly sucker-punched him. It happened on a Thursday, the day before their annual "Family Fun Day," which included eating breakfast out, ice skating, and a special dinner at a fancy restaurant. It also included a dance party in the middle, music and laughter, giggles and snuggles. He loved being the minority in a small sorority of four little girls and one special momma.

Family Fun Day was scheduled for a Friday, but Thursday changed everything. On December 20, Levi and his wife, Jennie, wrapped presents while their girls, Alivia, Lenya, Daisy, and Clover were at Grandma's house. After they finished tying on the last bow, they drove over to pick up the girls. When they pulled up to the house, Jennie's younger brother burst through the doors, yelling that Lenya, their five-year-old, wasn't breathing. Jennie's mom was trying to give Lenya her asthma treatment, but it wasn't working. Lenya looked up and saw her mommy enter the room just before her eyes rolled back and she lost consciousness. Levi administered CPR until the medics arrived. A few hours later, Lenya took her last breath.

This was not a good story. Levi wrote about his journey through a parent's worst nightmare in his book *Through the Eyes of a Lion*. Lenya had been nicknamed "Lenya Lion" for her ferocious personality and mane-like head of hair. I had a lump in my throat while reading Levi's story. He was raw and honest, yet also hopeful.

Toward the end of the book, Levi told about another family who had experienced a devastating loss. They had been flying thirty-eight thousand feet over the Pacific Ocean on their way to Honolulu. The couple's six-month-old baby boy was sleeping in his daddy's arms when they noticed he had stopped breathing. They desperately tried to wake him, to resuscitate him, to bring him back to life. They prayed. I'm sure others around them prayed. But when the airplane landed in Honolulu, the child was with the angels in the presence of God.

When a mutual friend told Levi the story, he gave the bereft father a call. The father told Levi that he was one of the first people he thought of after his son stopped breathing. They had never met, but the man had followed Levi's story about Lenya's homegoing. The man expressed gratitude for the call and told Levi that he and Jennie had been a template for him and his wife, teaching them how to navigate this tragedy. Levi prayed for him and offered the best encouragement he could. Then he hung up the phone and cried.

> I cried as I thought of the difficult days I knew lay ahead for that family. But I also cried out of a profound sense of humility and joy that came from knowing my pain had been used to give hope and courage to a desperate man while his son received CPR in the middle of the night on an airplane ride from hell. God used our suffering to bring a blessing to someone else. This is how God rolls. He put to use what he puts us through.[2]

One of the greatest ways God "puts to use what he puts us through" is by creating in us a deeper sense of compassion than we would have ever known without the trauma. The word *compassion* is derived from the Latin words *pati* and *cum*, meaning "to suffer with." That's what Levi offered this shattered family. That's what the preacher in the woods offered my guilt-ridden dad. *Compassion for brokenness comes from brokenness.* There's really no other way.

We hold the hands of weary friends, not as people who can fix their problems, but as people who understand their pain and "suffer with" them. *I'll walk through this with you. I get it. I may not understand the particulars of your struggle, but I do understand disappointment and heart-wrenching pain.* Only when we have experienced our own disappointment can we sympathize with the disappointment of others.

One of my greatest gifts from the loss of our child was a deeper compassion for women who struggle with infertility and loss. No one in my family had ever died before in my lifetime except my grandma, but her death was expected because she was old. However, when my baby died, that was not expected. When she died, something else in me was born—a deep-seated compassion for those who have prayed for years but not received the hoped-for reply, for the women whose dreams became nightmares, and for women who wanted answers but got none.

Paul wrote, "Praise be to the God and Father of our Lord Jesus Christ, the Father of compassion and the God of all comfort, who comforts us in all our troubles, *so that we can* comfort those in any trouble with the comfort we ourselves receive from God" (2 Corinthians 1:3–4, emphasis added). Another translation puts it this way: "[God] who comforts us in all our affliction, *so that we may be able* to comfort those who are in any affliction, with the comfort with which we ourselves are comforted by God" (v. 4 ESV, emphasis added).

The word translated "comfort" in this verse is the Greek word *parakalōn*. It comes from the root words *para* and *kaleo*, which mean "to call near, to invite, invoke." When we tell our stories to someone who is hurting, we come near to them and our words comfort them in a way that empty platitudes and easily recited Bible verses cannot. When we say, "Let me tell you what I've gone through," or "Let me tell you how I've failed," the hearer no longer feels isolated and alone in her struggle. In his book *Where Is God When It Hurts?*, Philip Yancey noted, "People who are suffering, whether from physical or psychological pain, often feel an oppressive sense of aloneness. They feel abandoned by God and also by others, because they must bear the pain alone and no one else quite understands."[3]

But suppose there is someone who understands. Suppose you are that someone, and you need to tell your story. When you share the comfort that you have experienced in your struggles, when you're honest and vulnerable with the facts, it lets the hearer believe there is hope for a better story.

God doesn't comfort us just to make us comfortable. He comforts us in order to make us comfort-*able*—able to comfort others. When we keep our stories to ourselves, we deny others the comfort that is ours to give.

No one can comfort a woman with cancer like a woman who has also heard the word *malignant* from a doctor's diagnosis.

No one can comfort the mother of a prodigal like a mother who has also worn her knees raw praying for her child to come home.

No one can comfort an abandoned wife like another woman who has also watched her husband walk out the door.

No one can comfort a woman who's struggling with the shame of an abortion like a woman who has experienced forgiveness and grace for her own.

No one can comfort a woman who's grieving over sexual sin like another woman who has been washed clean of the same.

When you tell your story, you give your listener the gift of knowing that she is not alone. She will breathe a sigh of relief that says, "I thought I was the only one. Finally, someone who understands."

When the #MeToo movement began with women telling their stories about inappropriate sexual advances and abuse, a splinter of a memory worked its way to the surface of my mind. I remembered a doctor in the building of my first job who came into my room, closed the door, and began to touch me inappropriately. I slapped him and demanded he leave, but I felt stupid for allowing him to close the door in the first place. It was a dirty little secret that I had buried. Funny thing about those secrets we bury; they seldom stay buried and often contaminate the soil of the soul in one way or another. I had never told anyone about that incident except my husband, but after the other brave women came forward, I thought, *Me too*. And in a strange way, I was comforted by that.

When someone hears your story, it may be painful and comforting at the same time. They might not have had the same experience that you had, but they do know what pain or shame feels like. It's not that the hearer is glad that you've experienced the abuse or the aftermath of a poor decision, but she does feel comfort in knowing she is not the only one who has messed up or been messed with.

God will bring people across your path who need someone who understands. *When a divine appointment meets a deliverance story, healing happens.* You may never know the *why* of your story, but you can experience the *how* of redemption when you share how God got you through.

Amazingly, no two people have the same story of God's redemptive work in their lives. Oh, sure, there's the basic "I was lost but now I'm found" that underscores the theme, but no one can tell the same story you were fashioned to tell. And each one of our stories reflects something unique and specific about God's character and the way he works in the lives of his people.

Think about all the stories of men and women in the Bible: Abraham, Sarah, Isaac, Jacob, Rebekah, David, Daniel, Mary, Martha. Each one of their stories teaches us something different about human struggle and God's character. Their lives were not interchangeable but used by God in a specific time for a particular purpose. The same is true for you and me. God has placed you here on earth at this particular time in history to tell your specific story—a story only you can tell (Acts 17:26). Your story matters because it is part of God's ultimate redemption story being played out in the lives of his people throughout history.

Has he given you joy in spite of ill-fated circumstances? Has he healed you from sickness, given you solace in a storm, counseled you in confusion, spoken to you through Scripture, delivered you from depression? Has he walked with you through addiction? Waded with you through the death of a child? Levi Lusko challenges each of us: "You have a unique and powerful voice, and as long as you have breath in your lungs, there is a microphone in your hands. How you use that platform you have been given is your choice every day."[4] Don't let anyone or anything silence the story you were meant to tell. It matters. It's powerful. It can affect future generations.

THE REASON FOR THE ROCKS

One of the saddest verses in the Bible is Judges 2:10: "After that whole generation had been gathered to their ancestors, another generation grew up who knew neither the LORD nor what he had done for Israel."

Back in the book of Exodus, God freed the Israelites from Egyptian slavery and sent them on their way to the promised land. But as we know, just because we've been set free doesn't mean that we will walk free. The first generation of slaves set free did not enter the promised land because of their ingratitude, unbelief, and disobedience. So, God waited for a second generation to rise up—a generation who would believe that God is who he says he is and will do what he says he will do.

Forty years after they first stepped foot in the wilderness, Joshua and Caleb led the people into Jericho to take possession of the land God had already given them. But first, the Israelites had to cross the Jordan River, which was at flood stage, the worst possible time to make such a trek. Nevertheless, the people decided to obey God's command rather than acquiesce to human reason. As soon as the priests leading the people put their feet in the water, the flow stopped twenty miles upstream and stood up in a heap. After the whole nation had crossed the river, God instructed Joshua to have twelve men gather twelve stones from the middle of the Jordan. Big stones. Heavy stones. Shoulder-hefting stones. Once they were on the other side of the promise, the stones became a monument to help the people remember what God had done. Joshua said to the people:

> "In the future, when your children ask you, 'What do these stones mean?' tell them that the flow of the Jordan was cut off before the ark of the covenant of the LORD. When it crossed the Jordan, the waters of the Jordan were cut off. These stones are to be a memorial to the people of Israel forever."

So the Israelites did as Joshua commanded them. (Joshua 4:6–8)

The Israelites obeyed to a point. Yes, they gathered the rocks. Yes, they set up a memorial. But, no, they did not tell their story. It stopped with that generation. Why didn't the next generation know the story? Because their parents didn't tell them. They didn't pass on the stories of how God brought them out of Egypt, through the Jordan, and into the promised land. Their stories died with them. The next generation had no idea.

Several years after the loss of our second child, I found an old Bible tucked in a cedar chest in my mom's attic. As I flipped through the pages, I stumbled upon a crude chart of our family tree written in my mom's flourishing hand. Listed were the names, dates of birth, and dates of death for my maternal and paternal great-grandparents and grandparents. Next, came my parents, my brother, Stewart, then me, and then my sister, Gloria Gale. My mind stopped for a beat. *My sister, Gloria Gale? Who's that?!* I never knew I had a sister named Gloria Gale. But there it was. A date of birth and a date of death. Digging through the old chest, I found pictures of a tiny casket, a child-sized grave, and an engraved tombstone.

I ran downstairs holding the opened Bible in my hand, walked over to my mom, pointed at the entry, and said, "What's this about? Who is Gloria Gale?"

"I had a baby girl when you were two years old," she said. "I guess you were too little to remember it. She was premature. She only lived a day."

"Why have you never told me I had a sister?"

"That was a long time ago," she said. "I don't really want to talk about it."

I was dumbstruck. Why didn't she want to talk about? Why didn't she tell me? More importantly, why didn't she share her painful story with me when I went through a similar experience of my own? The story had lain dormant, tucked between my dad's high school letter jacket and a piece of old cross-stitch, when it could have been a story that gave me hope at a time when I needed to know life would go on.

Oh, friend, your story matters. It matters to the people God brings across your path and to the generations that follow. Don't hide your story, no matter how sordid it may be. Nothing is ever wasted as long as we don't keep it to ourselves. People need to know how God brought you through your own personal Jordan River and onto the other side. If you don't tell your story, who will?

IF I'D ONLY KNOWN

One evening, my friend Pat Layton, who we met in chapter 6, was speaking at an event on the topic of forgiveness and restoration. At the close of her teaching, she invited attendees who were struggling with unforgiveness, guilt, or shame to come forward for prayer. A flood of tearstained faces congregated at the simple altar. Just when the crowd thinned and returned to their seats, a timid young woman and her mother braved their way down the aisle. Like a P.S. to a long letter, there was one more story to tell. The twenty-something woman clung to her mom as if she needed help putting one foot in front of the other.

"Will you stand beside me, Miss Pat?" she whispered. "I need to confess something to God and my mother, and I'm afraid it will break her heart as it has broken mine. But I can't carry the burden of this secret any longer."

Pat placed her arm around the young woman and assured her, "I'm here for you. I love you. God loves you. Go ahead. You can do it."

The woman told Pat what she was going to tell her mother and then turned to the woman she'd loved her entire life. In broken sobs, the young woman spoke in Spanish to her non-English-speaking mother and told her about an abortion she'd had several years earlier.

No one knew. Not even the father of the child. The secret had been the albatross of her existence, a heavy weight she carried all on her own. She just couldn't shoulder the burden any longer.

As the words of confession and contrition spilled from her lips, the mother began to rock back and forth, wailing as only a mourner could. Pat wasn't exactly sure what the daughter had said, but she had a pretty good idea. Neither she nor the daughter were surprised at the mother's reaction to the loss of her grandchild, but they were surprised at the words that followed. The daughter translated for Pat.

"Oh, my daughter, if only I had told you. I could have helped you. You see, when I was a young girl, I also had an abortion. I have been carrying the weight of this shame for years. If I had only had the courage to tell you my story, it might have given you the courage to change yours. I have never forgiven myself for what I did. And now here you are."

Men and women in the congregation looked on as the Holy Spirit began to fit the broken pieces of two women's lives into a dovetail of redemption. Mother and daughter prayed for forgiveness from God and from each other. Cleansing tears washed away the secret shame and two new chapters began.

What a wonderful story of redemption! But I wonder what would have happened if the mother *had* had the courage to tell her daughter the story years before. I wonder if her daughter would have made the same life-altering decision. Regardless of what might have been, they both experienced freedom when they told their stories that day.

Telling your story has the potential to set someone else free. Telling your story also has the ability to set you free—and to affect generations to come. That's why *your* story matters.

Chapter Nine

Speaking Up When You Tend to Clam Up

There is no greater agony than bearing
an untold story inside of you.

—Maya Angelou, *I Know Why the Caged Bird Sings*

She was a seven-year-old wisp of a girl with a Raggedy Ann lunch-box and pink tennis shoes. Melissa's bouncy brown hair swung as she skipped down the sidewalk on her way home from the school bus drop off. When the yellow doors cranked open, kids of all shapes and sizes spilled out onto the sidewalks with backpacks, lunch boxes, and rumpled clothes. The trek was only one block, but Melissa felt like a big girl to make the journey all by herself.

Melissa lived in a neighborhood teeming with kids. Big ones. Little ones. Tough ones. Tender ones. All of them looked for the grandfatherly man who sat at the end of his grown daughter's driveway to hand out candy and stickers to students headed home. They could count on Mr. Parks to be at his post, waiting in his green-and-white folding lawn chair. They liked him. He was nice.

One day, Melissa passed by Mr. Parks without the usual gaggle of children around her. "Hi, Melissa," he said. "I don't have my candy with me, but if you come into the garage with me, I'll get you some."

Melissa followed him. She walked in an innocent, trusting girl. She walked out scarred for life. Melissa didn't understand what was going on and didn't know what to do. Mr. Parks became a different person once the garage door slammed shut. He did things to her and made her do things to him that she never knew existed. When he was finished, he told her to come back the next day, and for some reason she can't explain, she did.

"In my mind, what I had done was so bad, I couldn't tell anyone," Melissa said. "And because it happened more than once, I felt like it really was my choice, my fault. That's what he told me. I felt dirty and filled with shame."

Children can't tell the difference between shame because of something done to them and shame because of something they've done. It all feels the same. *This must be my fault. I must be a bad person. I guess I'm not worth God protecting; God must not love me.* Little-girl thoughts such as these can become the filter for big-girl thoughts later in life. But none of these thoughts are true.

The elderly man stole Melissa's innocence, her trust in others, and her confidence in herself. It would be many years before what happened in that dark musty garage would come to light. Melissa stuffed the memories of forced acts of perversion down into the deep recesses of her heart. And for the next twenty-five years, shame ran like an undercurrent through her life, affecting every relationship she made and every decision she weighed. Silence was the force that kept her pain under lock and key.

In high school, Melissa became an overachiever to compensate for the emptiness she felt. She thought if she could pile on enough accolades, her achievements would somehow bury the shame. In her high school yearbook, clubs, activities, and honors filled the space beside her name and senior photo. No one knew the truth behind her bubbly personality. If they could see into her soul, they would have seen no bubbles at all—just flat emotions of resignation and regret.

When Melissa was in her thirties, God rattled the keys and beckoned her to walk free of the self-imposed bars that kept her bound. She realized how her childhood secret was affecting her adulthood relationships, particularly her marriage. Marital intimacy had been marred by the rough hands of a predator. The sexual abuse had twisted what God had intended for intimacy between a husband and wife into something it should not be. Just as the dirty yard tools, spiderweb-covered storage boxes, and smelly old tennis shoes had cluttered that dimly lit garage, shaming memories cluttered Melissa's mind. She was ready to clean it out. She was ready to tell someone.

Melissa went to a Christian counselor and shared her story of sexual abuse and molestation for the first time. Redemption was on the way.

TRADING IN YOUR GREEN STAMPS

When I was a little girl, my mom did her grocery shopping at White's Supermarket on the corner of Tarboro and Pearl Streets. Other grocery stores were close by, but only White's gave out S&H Green Stamps. On shopping days, I stood on tiptoes, bug-eyed, as the cashier pushed the buttons and rang up my mom's purchases. My mom lit up every time she heard the cha-ching, knowing that meant more stamps were on the way. After the cashier tallied the purchases, she pulled a lever and the register spit out two streams of stamps—large and small. We never put the stamps in books right away. Mom stuffed them in a brown paper bag and stored them in a cabinet over the oven.

About every six months, Mom pulled down the grocery bags swollen with S&H Green Stamps. "Okay, Sharon," she'd announce as she spilled the contents on the kitchen table. "Today we're going to paste the stamps in the books."

We'd make an afternoon of filling up the pages. The large stamps representing fifty cents spent went one to a page. Smaller stamps representing one cent spent went fifty to a page. I liked doing the big ones.

After six months of collecting stamps and hours spent pasting them in the books, my mom and I excitedly drove down to the S&H Green Stamp Redemption Center. With bags stuffed like a Loomis Fargo transfer, we plopped our day's work on the clerk's desk.

"Whatcha gonna get?" I'd ask Mom as we strolled up and down the aisles of housewares.

"I don't know," she'd reply. "But it'll be something good."

After much consideration, Mom would decide on a treasure such as an electric can opener, a steam iron, or a shiny set of stainless-steel mixing bowls. Oh, it was an exciting day when we traded in our stamps for a fabulous find!

I share this vintage memory because I love how it offers a simple picture of a complex concept called *redemption*. If you've been around in the church world much, you've probably heard that word a lot. I've already used it several times throughout these pages. But it's one of those words that can also be a little intimidating, to the point that we might pretend we know what it means even when we're a little fuzzy on the particulars.

So, what exactly does redemption mean? The dictionary defines *redemption* as "the action of saving or being saved from sin, error, or evil; the action of regaining or gaining possession of something in exchange for payment or clearing a debt; to exchange something such as a coupon for something else." Just to keep things simple, that entire definition can be boiled down to this: redemption means trading one thing for another.

We took our stamps to the center and traded them—redeemed them—for something better. Redemption is what God can do with the bad parts of our stories. When we lay the painful pages on the counter of trust, he exchanges them for something better: a story of triumph. But it requires our cooperation. He will never pry those stories from our clenched fists and force us to tell others how he brought us through the most shameful or difficult parts of our lives. He simply woos us into making the exchange. He knows it is only when we allow him to turn our pain into purpose that we will be truly free and fully healed.

UNEARTHING TREASURE FROM THE SOIL OF SILENCE

If Jesus had owned a store in his hometown, I think it would have been something like an S&H Green Stamp Redemption Center. His earthly ministry could be defined as getting people to trade in one thing for another and then encouraging them to tell about it.

Jesus was the master of not allowing the sick who had been made whole to slip away with an untold story. One of the best examples of this is in Jesus' encounter with the woman who had been bleeding for twelve years. She was identified not by her name, or what was right with her, but by what was wrong with her. My Bible identifies her as "the woman with the issue of blood."

Twelve years is a long time to live with a constant vaginal flow of blood. That's more than 4,380 days. She had sought the help of doctors, only to be left with no diagnosis and diminished resources. In those days, a woman with vaginal bleeding was considered ceremonially "unclean" and sequestered to her home. The house she lived in, the chair she sat in, the utensils she cooked with—all unclean. That meant she was permanently quarantined. I'm sure this woman longed for a human touch. A kiss. A hug. A pat on the back. But she was all alone.

One day, she heard that Jesus, the healer, would be passing

through town. I imagine that when she heard a ruckus outside her window, she grabbed her veil, covered her face, and pushed through the crowd to see him.

If I can just touch his clothes, I will be healed, she thought. I know it. I just know it. I can't let this opportunity pass me by. While unsure of herself, she was confident in him. Her faith overcame her fear and she forced her way through what had once intimidated her—the crowd.

When she got close enough, she extended her arm, leaned forward with an opened hand, and brushed her fingertips across the hem of his garment. Mark 5:29–30 tells us what happened next:

> Immediately her bleeding stopped and she felt in her body that she was freed from her suffering. At once Jesus realized that power had gone out from him. He turned around in the crowd and asked, "Who touched my clothes?"

The woman kept her eyes fixed on the ground, and I imagine a jumble of thoughts jounced in her mind. *I'm unclean and not supposed to be out in public. I'm not supposed to touch anyone. What am I going to do? If I remove my veil, people will recognize me. I'm not supposed to talk to a man in public.* She wanted to run, but her feet were rooted to the ground.

> "You see the people crowding against you," his disciples answered, "and yet you can ask, 'Who touched me?'" (v. 31)

Jesus ignored the disciples and continued panning the crowd—waiting as silence hung low. No one said a word. Finally, the woman couldn't hold it in any longer.

> Then the woman, knowing what had happened to her, came and fell at his feet and, trembling with fear, told him the whole truth.

He said to her, "Daughter, your faith has healed you. Go in peace and be freed from your suffering." (vv. 33–34)

Luke added an interesting comment in his account of this story:

Then the woman, seeing that she could not go unnoticed, came trembling and fell at his feet. *In the presence of all the people*, she told why she had touched him and how she had been instantly healed. (Luke 8:47, emphasis added)

"In the presence of all the people." Jesus didn't ask, "Who touched my clothes?" because he didn't know. He asked because he wanted the crowd to know. He wasn't going to let her slip away with a secret healing; he wanted her to tell her story to the entire crowd. He doesn't want you and me to slip away with a secret healing either. He wants us to speak up and share our story with others. And when we do, redemption waves the flag of victory over the worst chapters of our lives.

THE CROWNING OF COURAGE

Gina approached me during the free time at a women's retreat. She was a petite beauty with warm brown eyes and a tender smile. A brunette bob framed her heart-shaped face. Timidity tendered her steps. Caution shallowed her breath. She moved toward me as if she wanted to talk, but the words stuck in her throat.

"Gina, do you want to talk?" I asked as others cleared the room.

"I can't," she cried. "I am so ashamed."

"Do you want to tell me? You'll probably never see me again after this weekend, and I am a safe place."

"Yes," she continued. "I want to tell someone. This secret is killing me. I want to tell you, but I'm afraid. I've never told anyone."

I had been teaching on emotional and spiritual healing and the importance of telling our stories. Gina was ready to take a step, but it was a shaky one. Shaky ones are usually the most courageous.

We went to an outside deck and sat in rocking chairs pulled close together. Surrounded by the fall foliage of the Great Smoky Mountains and the sweet presence of God, Gina slowly began.

"My parents divorced when I was pretty young. My mom remarried when I was in high school. About six months after her husband moved into our house, he began making sexual advances toward me. Either my mother didn't notice what was happening, or she just refused to believe it. I felt alone and unprotected, and I sure didn't feel like anyone would believe me. So I did the only thing I thought I could do. I ran away. I stayed with a friend for a few days. I didn't tell her why I'd run away. But after a while, I knew I'd have to move on. I didn't have anywhere to go or any money to pay rent for an apartment.

"But then I met a woman who seemed to care about me. She told me about a way to make money, more money than I could ever make working at a minimum-wage job. She told me I might be repulsed at the idea at first, but that I'd get used to it in no time at all."

Even though I felt like I already knew the answer, I had to ask, "What did she want you to do?"

"Prostitution," slipped out of her mouth with years of pent-up pain.

We sat there a minute as she caught her breath and mustered up the courage to continue.

"I didn't get used to it. Every time I did it, part of me died. I didn't do it for long, just a few times, but I've never been able to forget the shame and how dirty I felt. Even though I'm now married, have two children, and a wonderful life, I still feel dirty. It was a long time ago, but it feels like yesterday. Nobody knows. My husband doesn't know; he always tells me how precious I am. If he knew, it would kill him."

We talked long that day. Much of the conversation was centered around the themes we've covered in this book. I reminded her about the story of the woman caught in adultery in John 8, and how Jesus forgave her sin. I reminded her about the amazing grace that wipes our slates clean. I reminded her about Paul's words of no condemnation for those who love Jesus. Nothing I said to Gina was new to her. She knew it all in her head. It was her heart that had trouble believing it could be true for her.

At the end of our time together, I asked, "Are you glad you told me?"

"Yes," she smiled. "Mainly because the way you are looking at me now is not any different than the way you were looking at me before you knew."

We hugged tight. And she walked away just a little lighter than she had walked in.

Telling your secret story may not be as hard as you think. In my experience, those who hear it will love you even more. People are drawn to vulnerability, respect transparency, and admire honesty, even when they are reluctant to take the plunge themselves.

Oh, sure, there may be some pious souls who are eager to throw the first stones. There will always be the big brother who frowns on the prodigal coming home. But I've noticed that they are few and far between. And if the big brothers (or sisters) do frown, *so what*? They're invited to the party too. Whether or not they accept the invitation is up to them. If anyone disapproves of us, we have this promise from God to hold on to: "Who will bring any charge against those whom God has chosen? It is God who justifies. Who then is the one who condemns? No one" (Romans 8:33–34).

If someone were to be aghast at how far I'd fallen before God raised me up, I'd simply say, "You don't know the half of it." I will not be a prisoner of people-pleasing or Potemkin performances. If I just lost you on that second one, let me explain.

Back in 1787, the empress Catherine the Great made a visit to a recent conquest, the Russian Crimea. In order to impress the empress,

Russian minister Grigory Potemkin erected fake villages along the desolate banks of the Dnieper River. Façades of settlements were erected far enough away from the riverbank so that the monarch and her traveling party could not tell that they were only flimsy veneers of buildings that were not really there. The glowing village fires were meant to comfort the monarch and her entourage as they surveyed the land, but the reality was her conquest was a barren and impoverished wasteland.

I don't want to be a Potemkin village, keeping people at a distance so I can appear to be better than I am. Come up close. Take a look. It might not be pretty, but it's real.

Listen, the devil does not want you to tell your story of what God has done in your life. He wants you to keep it bottled up and hidden away in the back of the pantry where no one can find it. He doesn't want you to tell how you traded in your anger and resentment for God's grace and forgiveness. How you traded in your feelings of condemnation and self-loathing for freedom and a new beginning. How you traded in your broken pieces for a beautiful masterpiece. *Don't do it,* he whispers. *They won't like you. They'll think badly of you. They'll reject you. Don't do it. You'll regret it. Once it's out there, it's out there. As long as nobody knows, you'll be accepted.*

But here's the truth: *If you listen to the wrong voice, you will make the wrong choice.* The devil will do everything he can to keep you silent. He knows that your willingness to place your story in God's holy hands will lead to full redemption, where, in the words of Beth Moore, "the pain is treated and turned around so thoroughly that it not only loses its power to do you harm but also gains the power to do some good."[1]

When I first felt God calling me to share with others how he had redeemed my past, I argued just a bit. "But God," I cried, "There are some things about my life I don't want to tell." And then I sensed him saying, *Would you rather people think well of you, or of me?*

At that point, I had a decision to make, and I've never regretted the transparency he's called me to. It could very well be that my mess could be the message that ushers in the miracle in someone else's life. If I refuse to speak up, God will choose someone else who will, and I will miss the blessing.

So, don't hide your story. Own it! Tell it! Rejoice in it! Realize that, no matter what has happened in your life, your lows, your disappointments, and your struggles can be the most compelling parts of your story. People will rally around you, and you will find love and connection in the process. If you are willing, your healed wounds can become the source of your greatest strengths.

God may not be calling you to tell your story in an auditorium full of strangers, but he is calling you to tell your story to someone. Look for that person you can trust with your heart—someone with whom you can feel totally exposed and completely loved at the same time. Then take the first step and tell your story.

I love the image Paul used when he wrote, "And we all, who with unveiled faces contemplate the Lord's glory, are being transformed into his image with ever-increasing glory, which comes from the Lord, who is the Spirit" (2 Corinthians 3:18). Unveiled faces. Unsealed stories. Unleashed power.

PLANTED SEED OR BURIED TREASURE?

Every redemptive story, like a raw seed, cannot realize its potential until it is planted in the heart of another human being. And a plant born of a seed will become a plant that bears more seeds.

One day, Jesus told a parable to a group of listeners. We've come to know it as the parable of the talents, but it is really more the parable of the three choices. Jesus used the parable to explain what the kingdom of heaven would be like.

> For it will be like a man going on a journey, who called his servants and entrusted to them his property. To one he gave five talents, to another two, to another one, to each according to his ability. Then he went away. He who had received the five talents went at once and traded with them, and he made five talents more. So also he who had the two talents made two talents more. But he who had received the one talent went and dug in the ground and hid his master's money. (Matthew 25:14–18 ESV)

When the master returned home, he was pleased with the two servants who had invested and doubled their talents. The master praised them by saying, "Well done, good and faithful servants!" But he was furious with the one who buried his one talent in the ground because of fear.

> You wicked and slothful servant! You knew that I reap where I have not sown and gather where I scattered no seed? Then you ought to have invested my money with the bankers, and at my coming I should have received what was my own with interest. So take the talent from him and give it to him who has the ten talents. (vv. 26–28 ESV)

A talent was a measure of weight. Some translations say "bags of gold" instead of the word *talent*. But Jesus was teaching us about far more than investing money. He was demonstrating what God expects us to do with what he has entrusted to us in every area of life. We can plant what he gives us and watch it grow, or we can bury it in the furrows of fear and walk away.

You may feel that you wasted part of your life because of failure, but the greater waste would be not telling what you learned from that failure. How God picked you up after you fell down. How God turned you around when you were headed in the wrong direction. How God drew you in when you had pushed him away . . .

I wonder if you have any bags of gold that are buried in the ground because of fear? Fear of rejection, embarrassment, or what others might think of you? *Fear has no choice but to leave the premises when you stand on the promises of God and say, "You are not welcome here."*

At this point in my journey, I've come to fear what would happen if I *did not* tell my story. Who would *not* be encouraged to take one more step, breathe one more breath, make it through one more day? Who would *not* know that she's not the only one? Who would *not* catch a glimpse of her future hope regardless of her painful past? And for that, I refuse to bury the talent that is my testimony when I have the choice to invest it into a human heart instead.

> *Fear has no choice but to leave the premises when you stand on the promises of God and say, "You are not welcome here."*

If you say yes to God and share your story, be prepared to hear these words from the Master: "Well done, good and faithful servant" (v. 21 esv). And remember, the opportunity to tell your story could happen anywhere, and you never know when your smallest investment will multiply in another's heart. This was exemplified in an email written to me by a woman named Mona about taking baby steps to tell others about how God had healed her from an abusive childhood:

My wound was raw and opened for nearly sixty years. It's healed now and I have a beautiful scar. I'm free from blaming myself and thinking myself unworthy of God's love and forgiveness. I am getting a small tattoo where only I will see it unless I'm barefooted. It may sound silly, but I've never felt more passionate about this. I've never been a fan of tattoos. However, it has opened the door to ministry twice already. The first time was with the person standing behind me when I was setting up the appointment. The tattoo artist asked me what word I wanted. I said, "Forgiven." The man behind me whispered, "Cool, I want that."

Whether we're talking about the man born blind, the prisoner set free, or the woman getting the word *forgiven* tattooed on her foot, each story stirs a longing in the heart of the listener. Isn't that why Jesus encouraged the ostracized woman with the issue of blood to tell her story? It wasn't to glorify the teller but to magnify the Healer so that others would say, "Cool, I want that."

LET ME TELL YOU A STORY

Let's go back to the story of Melissa, who tried to bury the shame of her molestation for so many years. Her healing was a beautiful progression of biblical truth replacing bald-faced lies. She realized that she was an innocent little girl when the abuse happened. It was not her fault. She was not forever marred by molestation but was cleansed by the blood of Jesus. She was not fatally damaged by a man but fearfully designed by God. The abuse was something that happened to her, but it was not her.

She also made a decision to forgive her abuser. "I wanted to hate him," she said. "What he did was the worst thing anyone could do to a little girl. But I chose to hate what he did and forgive the man who did it."

Sometime later, Melissa wrote an online devotion about her experience and her healing from sexual abuse. Hundreds of women contacted her. "Me too!" they cried. "It happened to me too." Many had never known even one other person who had experienced similar abuse until Melissa told her story. These women finally knew they were not alone.

One woman stood out among all the others—not because she had been molested, but because her daughter had. Susan emailed Melissa and asked if she could bring her twelve-year-old daughter, Hayley, to meet her. Melissa said yes.

Hayley was ten years old when her story of abuse began. After her parents divorced, she and her twelve-year-old brother spent every other weekend with her dad. Most weekends, they stayed at the apartment of her father's best friend and coworker. Her father stayed there, too, but was in and out, leaving the kids with this stranger.

Hayley was a cute little girl with long dark hair, sweet deep dimples, and a lean swimmer's frame. She was unsettled by her father's lanky friend and his scraggly hair, dirty T-shirt, baggy gym shorts, and breath that reeked of cigarettes. She felt rattled by the gun collection on the wall and the smoke that hung in the air. But she kept quiet. Their family had been a cauldron of chaos and she didn't want to cause more trouble.

And then it happened. With her brother in a back bedroom playing video games and her father asleep on the den floor, this man crept to the futon where Hayley slept and began sexually molesting her.

"I have guns," he whispered when he finished. "I know how to use them. I know where your momma works. I know where she parks her car. I know where you go to school. You better keep quiet." So, she did. Every time.

When her mom saw blood on her underwear, she confronted Hayley, but fear kept her quiet. Later, a physician confirmed Susan's suspicions. Hayley heard her momma's wails through the office walls when the doctor told her the news. A broken momma. A shattered child.

The abuser was arrested. Two years later, he was convicted and sentenced to twenty years in prison. It was a long two years of pre-trial testimonies and perpetual postponements. During that time and after, Hayley was hospitalized with suicidal tendencies and one suicide attempt. She was imprisoned in her shame. Tormented by her memories. Paralyzed by fear.

There is so much more to this story, but I want to take you to the day her mother, Susan, read Melissa's devotion. Hayley had wonderful counselors and excellent treatment after the man's arrest. They helped mend that broken heart with biblical truth and psychological therapeutic processes. But she needed something more. Hayley felt that she had no chance of ever having a Christian marriage and a normal family. In her eyes, her future was destined to consist of alcohol, drugs, and sexual promiscuity. That's what she thought became of people like her. In a word, Hayley felt hopeless.

After Susan read Melissa's devotion, she knew there was someone who could show her daughter that life could be different than what she expected. Hayley agreed to meet Melissa. As they sat down together, Melissa saw a twelve-year-old girl who wouldn't make eye contact or sit up straight. She seemed emotionally flat and lifeless. Hayley barely spoke. So Melissa did. She told Hayley her story in great detail. As Melissa shared the details, Hayley's eyes looked up. Teared up. And she finally spoke up.

When Melissa told Hayley her story, she saw the seeds go deep into the soil of this young girl's heart. Hayley knew that if Melissa could go through what she had gone through, and have a Christian husband, four children, and a normal life, then she could too. Melissa's story of healing and redemption was the catalyst for the resurrection of Hayley's hope.

Melissa's pain had gone full circle, with healing closing the loop. She had planted her seed in the fertile ground of Hayley's heart, and that seedbearing heart had produced more. Fourteen years later, a now grown-up Hayley told *her* story of molestation and redemption at a crowded women's retreat. Listeners who had suffered in silence came out of the woodwork. "Me too," they whispered. "Me too." Hayley's story of healing and redemption was the catalyst for resurrecting hope in the lives of several attendees. For both Melissa and Hayley, their worst chapters had indeed become their greatest victories. They traded one thing for another and got something so much better—redemption.

You may not have a bag of Green Stamps accumulating in a brown bag over your oven, but I'm guessing you probably do have some stories tucked away in a dark place just waiting to be told. Let me encourage you to get out those stories—the ones with lessons both big and small. Press them in the book called *Brave*, and experience redemption at its best as hope is born in the lives of others.

"Whatcha gonna get?"

"I don't know, but it'll be something good."

Chapter Ten

Disqualified? Says Who?

You are not merely the possessor and teller of a
number of stories; you are a well-written, intentional
story that is authored by the greatest Writer of
all time, and even before time and after time.

—Dan Allender, *To Be Told*

Chris was a curly-headed gregarious four-year-old the first time I met him. I was working as a dental hygienist at the time, and it was his first trip to the dentist. He squirmed a little. I laughed a lot. He had a great checkup, by the way. This little boy grew up to become my pastor, but that almost wasn't his story.

Chris's parents met while his mom was working at her dad's Rexall drugstore in uptown Charlotte. His dad drove a UPS truck and the Rexall was on his route. The girl behind the counter married the man behind the wheel and they became the Payne family. The couple had a baby girl they named Ashley, followed by twins, Chris and Amy. Chris's dad changed jobs and worked his way up the corporate ladder. His mother became a stay-at-home mom. The family was living the

American dream with three kids, a nice house in a friendly neighborhood, and a dog named Max.

Chris had a happy childhood. He loved his parents and was loved by them. They ate meals together, played sports, attended school activities, visited grandparents, and took vacations. Chris also remembers his parents having heated arguments that kept him a bit off balance. Yelling one minute and then periods of passive-aggressive silence the next. He wasn't sure why they fought, and for a kid, unanswered questions often lead to incorrect assumptions. *Is it my fault? Is my family broken? Will my parents get divorced?*

They weren't a churchgoing family during his early years. Christmas and Easter were about the extent of it. One day, an acquaintance invited his mom to a neighborhood Bible study. She thought it would be fun, so she purchased a set of colored pencils and a Kay Arthur Bible study on Romans. It wasn't too long before Chris's mom made a decision to follow Christ. The next weekend, she packed up her three children and a reluctant husband, and together they headed off to a Bible-teaching, evangelical church. A few weeks later, the reluctant husband walked the aisle and became a Christian as well.

Chris was nine years old when he prayed to receive Jesus in the quiet of his own bedroom. His two sisters followed shortly thereafter. Life was clicking right along for the Payne family, except for the parents' tenuous marriage. Several times, after a heated argument, Chris's dad left for a few days, but he always came back.

When the three teens went off to college, the couple had nothing left to tether their marriage. While they had been good parents, they had not been good partners. They became roommates, and not very good ones at that. After college, Chris moved home for a few months and noticed how little his parents communicated with each other. He wasn't surprised when they decided to get a divorce.

Chris was in seminary when his dad moved into a townhouse and his mom sold the family home to move into an apartment. Chris got married that same year. While in seminary, Chris started working in the pastoral care department at a large church. His job was to help restore hurting people to wholeness, guide others to make positive choices, and reestablish broken relationships. Pastoral care meant that his core responsibility was to nurture others through the peaks, valleys, and plateaus of life. A big job for a young man.

Chris was sitting at his desk one day when he got a call from another pastor at the church, Tom Kakadelis.

"Chris, I'm walking over to your office," he said. "Stay put."

A sick feeling churned in Chris's gut. The weekend before, he, his wife, and his siblings and their spouses had spent a weekend in the Smoky Mountains with their dad. His dad had gone through a difficult year, experiencing a car accident followed by a job loss. The weekend seemed like it had bolstered his dad's spirits. They took long walks, played board games, engaged in meaningful conversations, and laughed a lot. They couldn't have asked for a better weekend together.

However, the next day, this day, Chris called his dad and it went straight to voicemail. All day, Chris waited for his dad to return his call. He never did. Something was off.

Tom walked into Chris's office with a policeman in tow. Tom was visibly shaken. The policeman was somber.

"Is my dad dead or alive?" Chris asked.

"He's dead," Tom replied.

Chris later discovered that his dad had walked across the street from his townhouse into an open field, placed a gun to his head, and pulled the trigger. When Chris stepped into his dad's home, he saw sticky notes throughout, leaving instructions for what to do once he was found. This had not been an impulsive decision but a deliberate and premeditated one.

The entire family went through all the stages of grief. Question marks filled the margins of their tearstained pages. But Chris had a few questions to grapple with that his siblings did not. *How can I be a pastor when I can't even help my own family? How did I miss the signs? Dad told me everything—why didn't he tell me this? Should I continue in ministry when I feel like I've already failed? Who am I fooling? How can I keep doing this?*

Chris felt disqualified from ministry, but God began to show him that he now had qualifications a seminary degree could never provide.

Two years earlier, Chris had been a student in a seminary class called Introduction to Pastoral Ministry. He remembers a student who raised his hand and asked the professor, "What is your best advice on how to be a good pastor?"

"Empathy," the professor replied. "Have empathy."

Then Chris raised his hand. "How do you get empathy?

With a trace of sad knowing in his eyes, the wise older man replied, "Suffer."

Chris now understood. Empathy isn't something you learn; empathy is something you live.

This was not a good story. If he could, Chris would tear this chapter from the narrative and send it through the shredder. But he can't. If he could, he would rewrite the story with a different ending. But he can't. All he can do is gather the fractured pieces of his family's life and place them into the hands of the One who fashions and fits the fragments together for good. And even though he didn't choose it, Chris knew that God would use it.

Twenty years later, I sat with Chris and talked about how God was using him in ways he could never have imagined. He shared story after story of literally hundreds of men, women, boys, and girls who have come to him because they know he understands. He's taken the hand of hurting people on the brink of suicide, as well as those left behind by others who've succumbed.

Chris is a living example of the biblical charge to use what we've gone through to comfort others. As 2 Corinthians 1:3–4 says, "God is our merciful Father and the source of all comfort. He comforts us in all our troubles so that we can comfort others. When they are troubled, we will be able to give them *the same comfort* God has given us" (NLT, emphasis added).

It's the phrase "the same comfort" that gives me pause. People come to Chris because they need *the same comfort*. They don't go to a trusted friend or even their own pastor.

Yes, pain is pain, but when you're going through certain trials, tragedies, or traumas, there is no greater salve than to be with someone who is on the other side of the *same* trouble you're experiencing. Chris has earned the right to speak into hearts that someone who hasn't experienced the same kind of loss has not. He has become a plank the broken can walk across to traverse the chasm of suffering. The broken and bruised come to Chris because, well, he's qualified.

DISQUALIFIED BY THE WORLD, QUALIFIED BY GOD

Chris struggled with feeling disqualified because of the actions of another he was unable to intercept. But what if it is *your own* actions that leave you feeling disqualified and emotionally disabled? If you flip through the Bible, you'll see a long list of men and women the world would deem disqualified. And yet, God used this bunch of misfits who made mistakes, had missteps, and were easily misled.

King David had an affair with his next-door neighbor and then had her husband killed. Yet, the Bible describes him as a man after God's own heart and the greatest king who ever lived.

Abraham took some bad advice from his wife and slept with her maidservant to produce an heir rather than wait for God's promise. And yet, he became the father of the Hebrew nation.

Jacob deceived his father and stole his brother's birthright and blessing. And yet, God chose him to be the father of the twelve tribes of Israel.

Moses took the matter of freeing the Israelites into his own hands by killing an Egyptian and hiding him in the sand. And yet, God chose him to lead two million Israelites out of bondage and into freedom.

Rahab turned tricks as a prostitute for a living. And yet, God chose her to play a leading role in the tumbling of Jericho's walls and the taking of the promised land.

The writer of Hebrews capped off the list of the great men and women of faith with this statement:

> And what more shall I say? I do not have time to tell about Gideon, Barak, Samson and Jephthah, about David and Samuel and the prophets, who through faith conquered kingdoms, administered justice, and gained what was promised; who shut the mouths of lions, quenched the fury of the flames, and escaped the edge of the sword; *whose weakness was turned to strength.* (Hebrews 11:32–34, emphasis added)

God used weak men and women to change the world. That doesn't mean we don't try to strengthen our weakness. But it does mean that even our best efforts will not come close to what God's Spirit can do through a willing vessel, no matter how cracked it is.

Each one of these people came face-to-face with their own weakness, and even though Paul's line "When I am weak, then I am strong" (2 Corinthians 12:10) was penned a few thousand years later, they knew the truth of that verse by heart.

And then there's Peter. He made many mistakes during his time with Jesus, and it seems he made the worst ones when it mattered most.

Just before Jesus went to the cross, he had one last supper with the disciples. He turned to Simon Peter and said,

"Simon, Simon, Satan has asked to sift you as wheat. But I have prayed for you, Simon, that your faith may not fail. And when you have turned back, strengthen your brothers."

But he replied, "Lord, I am ready to go with you to prison and to death."

Jesus answered, "I tell you, Peter, before the rooster crows today, you will deny three times that you know me." (Luke 22:31–34)

And he did.

The third time Peter denied that he knew Jesus, Jesus was looking right at him. Then Peter went outside and wept bitterly. I don't know about you, but I've gone outside and wept bitterly a few times myself.

Peter's faith didn't fail, but his courage did. How do I know that? Because Jesus prayed that it wouldn't. Satan tried to snuff out Peter's faith, but it was merely eclipsed for a moment. That can happen to any of us, and probably will. Peter fell in the dirt of doubt, but he rose again a few days later. That, too, can happen to any of us, and hopefully will.

Peter felt disqualified because of his failure and went back to doing what he did before he knew Jesus—fishing for fish rather than fishing for men. Feeling disqualified will do that to a damaged or disappointed soul. However, Peter wasn't disqualified at all. He just felt he was.

Sometime after Jesus' resurrection, Peter and John were fishing on the Sea of Galilee. From shore, a man called out to them and told them to cast their empty nets on the other side of the boat. Once they did, an overflow of fish filled the nets. That's when Peter realized the man who had called out to them was Jesus. Peter immediately jumped out of the boat and swam to shore, where Jesus had breakfast waiting.

When they had finished eating, Jesus asked Peter three times, "Peter, do you love me?" Peter said, "Yes, Lord, I love you." To which

Jesus replied, "Feed my sheep; take care of my lambs; feed my sheep" (John 21:15–17).

Peter remembered Jesus' prediction that he would deny him three times. He remembered Jesus' promise to pray his faith would not fail. But Peter had forgotten Jesus' words, "When you have returned, strengthen your brothers." So, Jesus reminded him.

What did Jesus mean when he said, "strengthen your brothers"? I think he was reminding Peter to tell his story. His failure did not *dis*qualify him but uniquely *qualified* him to encourage his companions when they fell as well. I don't know about you, but Peter's story encourages me even today.

When we make a mess of our lives, we tend to try to write ourselves out of the story. *I've fallen too far. I've done too much. I'm disqualified from telling anyone anything about Jesus.* But God keeps writing our names back into the story. "When you have returned, strengthen your brothers."

It's easy to go back to doing what we've always done after a time of failure. That's certainly what Peter did when he took up the net. We falsely believe that what we've done is inexcusable and wrongly deem ourselves unusable—that our botched-up storyline is beyond redeeming. But it's these words we need to hold on to: "When you have returned, strengthen your brothers." You are now qualified to know what you're talking about. Your trials give you credibility you otherwise would have never had.

MISCALCULATIONS AND MISEVALUATIONS

My son, Steven, was in the ninth grade when I turned in the manuscript for my book *Being a Great Mom, Raising Great Kids*. I should have waited until he was in the tenth grade.

That fateful morning, I placed my neatly printed pages in a padded enveloped, prayed a blessing over the bundle, and then dropped a year of hard work in the mail slot at the post office. When I returned home, my phone was ringing. It was Steven.

"Hey, Mom, I'm calling to let you know that I'm in the principal's office. I got caught stealing in the lunchroom. You need to come to the school."

I sped to the school, stomped down the hall, and opened the principal's door. There sat this strange person wearing my son's clothes slumped sheepishly in a chair. Steven got five days of in-school suspension, which was the least of his worries.

After I got him home, I wanted to climb back into that mailbox and GET THAT MANUSCRIPT OUT OF THERE! *Who did I think I was writing a book on parenting? What was I thinking? What an idiot! I am so disqualified!* I called the publisher and told them the story, giving them an out. The vice president just said with a smile in his voice, "Welcome to the real world."

I felt the incident had disqualified me. God said it didn't. Looking back, I needed that struggle. Steven had been an easy kid. If I was going to be telling anybody anything about raising kids, I needed to hit a wall, climb over it, and find Jesus cheering for me on the other side.

Okay, you might be thinking, *So what, your kid stole from the lunchroom. I've stolen someone's husband. I've been arrested. I've traded sex for money. I've had abortions.* We could compare mistakes and missteps all day long. But the devil taunts us with the same word: *disqualified.* Go ahead, say the word aloud. Can you hear the serpent's hiss? What most of us think disqualifies us is often what qualifies us to know what we're talking about.

Don't let the devil tell you that your past pain disqualifies you from your present calling. There's nothing he would like more than for you to hold an audition in your head and stamp a big REJECT across your own forehead. The audition is canceled. You got the part.

The Bible tells us, "For we are God's handiwork, created in Christ Jesus to do good works, which God prepared in advance for us to do" (Ephesians 2:10). The Greek word translated "handiwork" is *poēma*, which also means masterpiece, workmanship, epic poem. We need to get this. God created us for a purpose and a plan before we were born. He even marked out the times and places we would live (Acts 17:26). How silly to think that his plans could be altered or negated because of something we've done, or something that has been done to us. We'll never hear God say, "Oops, I didn't see that coming." God does the qualifying. Not me. Not you. Not anyone sitting in the stands.

Consider Paul's words to the Corinthians: "It is not that we think we are qualified to do anything on our own. Our qualification comes from God. He has enabled us to be ministers of his new covenant" (2 Corinthians 3:5–6 NLT). It is all about God from start to finish. My earthly qualifications to do what God has called me to do are irrelevant.

When I first felt God calling me to share my story in a bigger way, I argued like Moses at the burning bush. *Who am I that I should go? Suppose they don't believe me? Can't you please call someone more qualified . . . like Aaron?*

You know where those thoughts originated? With the enemy. Let's consider how to reject those lies and replace them with truth.

DEFEATING THE LIES OF THE ENEMY

If we let him, the devil will take the wrong we've done—or had done to us—and try to convince us it's who we are. He slaps a label on us, and before we know it, we're monogramming it on our shirt pocket. In her book *Unglued*, Lysa TerKeurst said this: "Those labels start out as little threads of self-dissatisfaction but ultimately weave together into a straitjacket of self-condemnation."[1] The truth is, your past is something you did or had done to you; it is not who you are. Just because you failed does not mean you *are* a failure. Just because you were abused does not mean that you are damaged goods. Whatever is in your past does not disqualify you.

We're in trouble any time we slap labels on our hearts that say, *That's just who I am. I'm an adulterer. I'm a rape victim. I'm a domestic abuse survivor. I'm a cheat. I'm a child-abuse victim.* Anytime we take a painful event or detrimental decision and make it the whole of our identity, we're living a lie. One sliver of a story does not define the entire narrative.

Your past is something you did or had done to you; it is not who you are.

Although I became a Christian when I was fourteen, the lies of the enemy—that I wasn't good enough and never would be good enough—followed me into my new life in Christ. They created limitations in my life. They were the barbed wire that fenced me in and kept God's best at bay.

I was free, but I didn't live free. I carried the chains around with me out of pure habit and lack of biblical knowledge. Oh, I understood that I was going to go to heaven when I left this earth, but I was stumped about what I was supposed to do until I got there. I felt that I was always a disappointment to God, and I was certainly a disappointment to myself. I tried the best I could to be the best I could be, but I always fell short. I settled into a stagnant faith, a safe faith, a stuck faith with other defeated believers who also saw themselves through a filter of past sins and failures, rather than through the lens of their new identity as a child of God.

Childhood echoes of "You're so ugly" and "What's wrong with you?" and "You can't do anything right" left me feeling congenitally flawed. I sat in Bible study groups like someone in a hospital waiting room: hoping for the best but expecting the worst. My greatest fear was that I'd be no closer to being free of the insecurity than I was before the study began.

When I was in my midthirties, I sat under the teaching of an older woman in my church, Mary Marshal Young. She opened my eyes to the truths in Scripture about who I was, what I had, and where I was (my position) as a child of God. I had read those verses scattered through Scripture before, but when she encouraged me to cluster them altogether into one list, God began a new work in my heart.

> *You are a saint.*
> *You are chosen.*
> *You are dearly loved.*
> *You are holy.*

These truths were right there on the pages of my Bible in black and white, and a few in red.

> *You are reconciled through Christ's life.*
> *You are justified by Christ's blood.*
> *You are free from condemnation through Christ's death.*
> *You have the mind of Christ.*
> *You can do all things through Christ.*

I knew the verses were the infallible Word of God, but I felt rather squeamish hearing them, reading them, believing them for myself.

They didn't feel right.

They didn't sound right.

They made me downright uncomfortable.

And while I was studying about my true identity, the devil taunted me with accusations. *Who do you think you are? A saint? Are you kidding? This stuff might be true for some people, but it certainly is not true about you.*

It's not that we knowingly tell ourselves lies about who we are. It's that we've embraced them as truth, and they become a warm snuggly for the soul. It is comfortable to get wrapped up in self-pity or victimization. We don't have to take responsibility for our future. It's always someone else's fault. Listen, this might sound harsh, but I'm talking to myself here too. I can throw some of the best pity parties around, until I realize that no one else is showing up. As a matter of fact, those invited to my pity parties run in the opposite direction. And if I'm having a party no one wants to come to, I need to stop and consider why.

One day, I sensed God asking me an important question—one he is asking you right now. *Who are you going to believe? The enemy or me?*

Finally, I was sick and tired of being sick and tired. "God, I'm going to believe I am who you say I am. I don't feel it. I can barely think it. But I'm going to believe your Word is true, for me and about me." See, we can't have a better story if we wrongly define the character we play in the narrative. Do you need to rename your character from victim to victor? From child of divorce to child of God? From tarnished to refined? From rejected by the world to chosen by God? From ruined to restored?

Author Seth Godin wrote, "People don't believe what you tell them. They rarely believe what you show them. They often believe what their friends tell them. They always believe what they tell themselves."[2] So start today. Tell yourself the truth and watch God begin to change the way you think.

The devil wants you to believe that you are a no-good, worthless excuse for a Christian who has no power, no victory, and no joy. He knows that you have been set free by the blood of Jesus, and he will try everything he can to keep you from believing it and walking in it. He knows that you've been qualified by God to do all he's called you to do. He capitalizes on every hurt, magnifies every mistake, and punctuates every promise with a question mark rather than an exclamation mark.

He tries to hoodwink you into thinking that you're no different now than you were before you came to Christ. He's lying.

You are who God says you are, whether or not you feel like it. However, the way you see yourself will determine the way you live. It is up to you to relentlessly protect your identity and not allow the enemy to steal your confidence—which he will try to do every chance he gets.

Here are four steps you can take to defeat the lies of the enemy when he tells you that you're disqualified or unqualified to do what God is calling you to do.

Recognize the Enemy's True Identity

We've got that, right? The enemy is not really the person who hurt you, the parent who abandoned you, the husband who left you, the friend who deceived you, or the stranger who maligned you. The real enemy is the devil himself. He will do everything he can to keep God's children from walking in power and purpose. Here are just a few of the things the Bible tells us about the enemy.

He is a schemer. Paul wrote, "We are not unaware of [Satan's] schemes" (2 Corinthians 2:11).

He is a liar. In fact, Jesus actually called him "the father of lies" (John 8:44). That means that all lies began with him. He uttered the first lie recorded in the Bible (Genesis 3:4–5), and he continues to taunt us with lies today.

He is a thief. Jesus said, "The thief comes only to steal and kill and destroy" (John 10:10).

He is an opportunist. The Bible tells us that after the devil finished tempting Jesus in the wilderness, he "left him until an opportune time" (Luke 4:13).

This is the enemy's true identity. This is who we're listening to when we choose to accept the lies about ourselves rather than believe God's truth. If we don't know who we're fighting, we can't win the battle for our thought life.

Recognize the Lies

Preacher D. L. Moody once said, "The best way to show that a stick is crooked is not to argue about it or spend time denouncing it, but to lay a straight stick alongside it."[3] Listen to what you are telling yourself about yourself. Does it line up with God's Word, or is it as crooked as an arthritic toe? *I'm so stupid. I can't do anything right. I'm such a loser. I'm damaged goods. I'm disqualified and unqualified to do what God's calling me to do.* I can almost smell the sulfurous breath of the evil one. Those statements are not true about you. Don't allow the enemy to whisper lies into your mind and then claim them as truth.

Reject the Lies

Once you recognize the lies, then reject the lies. Say it out loud if you have to: "That's not true." Declare it. Remember who you're talking to—the enemy. Say it like you mean it. Like a cowgirl lassoing a runaway bull, sling the rope of truth around the scrawny neck of that lie and drag it to the ground where it belongs. You have divine power on your side. The apostle Paul wrote:

> For though we live in the world, we do not wage war as the world does. The weapons we fight with are not the weapons of the world. On the contrary, they have divine power to demolish strongholds. We demolish arguments and every pretension that sets itself up against the knowledge of God, and *we take captive every thought to make it obedient to Christ.* (2 Corinthians 10:3–5, emphasis added)

Take any lying thoughts captive. Throw them down. Stomp on them a few times just for good measure.

Replace the Lies with Truth

Once you've recognized and rejected the lies, replace the lies with truth. Allow God to baptize you in the affirmation that you are his child, whom he loves, and with you he is well pleased. The thoughts you consume will consume you—so keep your thoughts focused on truth. It is not what you've done that determines your identity; it is what Jesus has done for you.

What are you telling yourself about yourself? That you are qualified by the blood of Jesus, or that you are disqualified because of mistakes, failures, abuses, and misuses? The way you answer that question will determine whether or not you will have a better story than the one you're currently experiencing. Victim or victorious? You get to choose. Realigning what you think about your true identity to match what God says about you changes everything. You cannot act differently than you think. If you think you are disqualified, then you will shrink back when God is calling you to step out.

Have you ever told yourself that you are any of the following?

- Not good enough
- Not smart enough
- Not strong enough
- Unlovable
- Unaccepted
- Unredeemable
- Inadequate
- Insignificant
- Incomplete
- Worthless
- Helpless
- Powerless

Guess what? Those are all lies. Every one of them. How do I know? Because if you know Jesus Christ as Savior and Lord, you are equipped by God, empowered by the Holy Spirit, and enveloped by Jesus Christ. As a matter of fact, this is who God says you are.

- You are chosen (Ephesians 1:11).
- You are valuable (Matthew 6:26).
- You are dearly loved (Colossians 3:12).
- You are beautiful (Ephesians 2:10).
- You are anointed (1 John 2:20).
- You have been appointed (John 15:16).
- You are free of condemnation (Romans 8:1).
- You are washed, justified, and sanctified through Christ (1 Corinthians 6:11).
- You are holy in God's sight, without blemish and free of accusation (Colossians 1:22).[4]

You know, all those accumulated verses about my identity in Christ were not new to me all those years ago when Mary Marshall Young suggested I make a list. Perhaps they are not new to you either. I had read them before and had even memorized a few. But I didn't believe they were true for me. Not really. I would never have admitted that to anyone—not even to myself. I'd smile and say "amen" with the best of them. But when the rubber of the truth hit the road of adversity, I moved those verses into the category of nice gestures on God's part, rather than the bedrock truth of who I really was.

One of the most difficult battles you will ever face is the battle for your thought life. That's why Scripture tells us, "Do not conform to the pattern of this world, but be transformed by the *renewing of your mind*" (Romans 12:2, emphasis added). It is so easy to say, "That's just the way I am," and ignore the fact that it's just the way your mind has been programmed to be. No one is "just the way they are." "Just the way I am" can be replaced with "That's just the way I was" by renewing the mind and reconstructing the neurological pathways in the brain.

What are you telling yourself about yourself? About your current or past circumstances? Whatever you are telling yourself, you will believe it. Make sure your truth is God's truth.

Every time God reveals a new truth about your identity, choose to receive the truth into your mind so you *know* it. Next, receive that truth into your heart so you *believe* it. Then adjust your life to apply the truth so you *act* on it. Know the truth, believe the truth, and act on the truth. That is how to reject the lies of the enemy.

A STORY I WAS NOT
EXPECTING TO HEAR

I've said it before but it bears repeating: *The very pages I would previously have wanted to rip out of my story have now become my greatest treasures.* Without the struggles, I might have a head knowledge about the redemptive power of Jesus, but I would have never had the experiential knowledge that the pain so sweetly instilled within me.

You are more than the splinter of your story that you hate most. You are exactly who God says you are, and the redeemed parts of your story are among the most powerful tools God has given you. That's a truth I know from personal experience and also from witnessing it in countless lives.

One weekend I was speaking at a women's event in Virginia. The women's ministry coordinator was a vivacious powerhouse who loved Jesus. She raised her hands in worship, sang like no one but God was listening, and led her team with excellence. It was evident by the hugs and cheek kisses that Lisa was a spiritual mentor and confidant to many women in her church.

During lunch, I very nonchalantly asked, "Lisa, what's your story? How did you come to know Jesus?" As she spoke, I put down my fork. Her story was better than any lunch could ever be. Pull up a chair and listen in as Lisa tells her story.

I was born into a family with three older brothers. I don't remember much of my early years, but one of my earliest childhood memories is of me when I was five years old standing over a bridge and thinking, *If I fell over this bridge into the river and disappeared, no one would ever care.* I always felt like something was wrong with me—like I was a misfit or an irregular.

I remember my mother saying to me, "What's wrong with you?!"

As a little girl, I thought, *I don't know, but I know it must be something!* I felt uncomfortable in my own skin—like I didn't belong, wasn't accepted, wasn't lovable or valuable.

When I was thirteen, I took my first drink of wine. I actually downed three bottles in one sitting. It felt good. I felt good. All my insecurities were gone. I lost my virginity when I was fourteen and smoked marijuana for the first time that same year. For the next twenty-eight years, I chased after anything and everything to numb my pain. Whether it was food, exercise, shopping, men, alcohol, or drugs, I sought after anything that would transport me into a different world for a while and fill the void in my soul.

After high school, I worked in Washington, DC, at a law firm. But that didn't last very long as I was fired for falsifying records. After that, I went to work as a bartender. My alcohol and drug use began to escalate, and I began to plummet. I moved in with a man who beat me up on a regular basis. I felt I deserved it.

One night, I reached the end of my rope and tried to kill myself with sleeping pills. For some reason, I called my mom to say goodbye, and she alerted the rescue squad. Even though I spent time in the psychiatric ward, I left the hospital just as lost and confused and desperate as when the ambulance had brought me in.

Cocaine is very expensive, and I needed a way to support my habit, so I became a prostitute on the streets of Washington, DC. With every trick, a piece of me died. Pretty soon, I became numb to it all. Amazingly, I was arrested, not for prostitution, but for writing bad checks. My attorney got me out of jail and into a treatment program. This was the beginning of a long road to recovery, but the reason I am alive today is because I met someone. It wasn't a lawyer, a mentor, or the man of my dreams. His name is Jesus Christ, and he's the one who set me free.

I sat there with a lump in my throat, tears in my eyes, and love for my Savior pounding in my heart. I had made a simple request, "Tell me your story," and gotten so much more than I expected.

It would have been so easy for Lisa to feel that her life as a law-breaking, drug-addicted prostitute would have disqualified her from becoming a women's ministry director of a church. But you see, her past actually *qualified* her for ministry. Redemption does that. Flipping your story does that. It makes you believable. It makes Jesus conceivable.

While you might look at your past as a stumbling block, God sees your past as a stepping-stone. The redeemed trauma of your past, no matter how you received it, can become the springboard for a greater story that God can mightily use.

Chapter Eleven

Lens One or Lens Two?
Which Is Better?

Gratitude is the antibiotic of the soul to cure a variety
of the world's ills. It changes the lens through which
we see our circumstances in our little slice of time.

—Sharon Jaynes, *A Sudden Glory*

Patricia was twenty-one when she met the charming Rodney. She was visiting her cousin when they ran into each other at the mall. *Boy, is he handsome*, she thought. Patricia had heard rumors of his partying bad-boy reputation and knew, as a Christian, that she should keep her distance. But secretly, she hoped he would call.

Rodney was intrigued with the cute visitor in town, and when he called to ask Patricia out on a date, she said yes. Everything about Rodney was contrary to her family values and faith, but she felt the tug.

Rodney felt the tug as well. Patricia was a challenge to Rodney, and he liked that. She was unlike any other woman he had notched on his bedpost, and he sought to win her over.

After their first date, Rodney sent Patricia special-delivery letters, bought her expensive gifts, and took her to showy restaurants. The lavish displays of attention were new to this young woman who had lived under the protective care of a loving family. And even though her head told her to run in the opposite direction, her heart told her to stay. Patricia believed Rodney when he told her he had been saved at his grandmother's church. Even though he never went to church on Sundays or showed any outward evidence of being a believer, she turned a bedazzled blind eye to his drinking and partying. She closed her ears to the alarm bells going off in her head and looked the other way— avoiding the "Do Not Enter" signs written all over his handsome face.

When it became apparent to Rodney that the only way he was going to win her over completely was to marry her, he proposed. She said yes.

Patricia's parents knew of Rodney's reputation. They and several other adults cautioned Patricia about moving forward. "But I love him," she naïvely replied. "I think he'll change."

The closer the wedding date came, the louder the voice of the Spirit in her said, *Run.* At one point, Patricia spent several hours with a Christian counselor who cautioned her about marrying someone so different from herself—someone with a totally different belief system and moral compass. She knew what she was hearing was truth. It was not God's best for her to marry this man at this point in his life. But she had convinced herself it was too late. The invitations had been mailed, the wedding dress altered, and the venue secured. Patricia felt trapped. She wiped away the tears, took a deep breath, and went ahead with the wedding—doubts riding on the train of her beautiful dress. At that point, she thought she could save him.

If I could stop right here and have a chat with you, I think you'd tell me, "Hey, I've heard this story before. Only the names are different." And you're right—this story is nothing new. It's a rerun. A reprint. A sad classic. An updated version of an old manuscript. Good girl meets bad boy. It happens all the time. But Patricia is not like any character in any story I've ever read or seen. Let's keep going.

It only took a few weeks before Rodney said he wasn't happy and that he'd made a mistake. Patricia wasn't happy either. Before their third-month anniversary, Rodney went to a fraternity party at his college alma mater for a weekend of letting loose and drinking up. When he came home, they both agreed to separate. Rodney had played with Patricia's heart like she was a stuffed teddy bear to be won at a carnival ring-toss booth. He won the prize, but then decided he didn't want it after all.

A few weeks after separating, he begged to come home. Patricia took him back. They decided to stay together and work on the marriage. "I had made a commitment to God," Patricia said, "and I was going to keep that commitment as best I could. I forgave him, and we tried again."

Over the next two decades, Rodney left the marriage three more times—once before their three children were born, and twice after. They lived through nineteen different homes in multiple cities, revolving jobs, rumored affairs, cycles of financial plenty followed by financial deficiency. Rodney often told Patricia that she wasn't pretty enough, sexy enough, or smart enough. He poked fun at her, degraded her, and expected her to have sex no matter what went on during the day. When he lost a job, which happened often, he blamed it on her. Eventually, after twenty-three years, Rodney packed his bags for the last time and left. The divorce was final the following year. That long chapter was over.

Friends, this is not hearsay or an email I received from a random reader. Patricia is one of my dearest friends. I lived this story with her. I couldn't understand why she didn't leave him. To me, she seemed stuck, but Patricia didn't feel she was stuck at all. For her, it was a decision to stay. She knew she had biblical grounds for divorce and could leave at any time, but she chose not to.

Just the other day I asked her, "Patricia, why did you stay with Rodney all those years?"

"I prayed and never felt a peace about leaving," she said. "I knew God was bigger than any problems we had. I prayed that Rodney would see Jesus through me, but he didn't. Or maybe he did and his rebellious spirit flat out refused to accept it. But I have no regrets. If I had not married Rodney, I would not have the strong faith that I have today. If life had been easy, I think I would have a flabby faith that could maybe quote Scripture but not necessarily believe it. I would have grown spiritually sloppy rather than spiritually strong. Because I had to depend on God to provide for me and my children, especially emotionally, I know God as my provider. Because I had to depend on God's love for me when I didn't get it from Rodney, I know the depths of his love for me. Because I had to stand on God's Word when the world around me was falling apart, I know the Rock on which my feet are planted. Had I not gone through those difficult years, I would not have the trust in God that I have today. He gives me life. He is my life."

I don't tell this story to stir up conflicting opinions on whether or not someone should stay or leave in a similar situation, but to wake up the desire to look at life from a better lens. Patricia did not get stuck looking through the lens of regret and pain, allowing bitterness to color the rest of her life. She flipped the lens to discover the blessings, allowing joy to color the remainder of her days. That's something we can all do.

We've all been hurt by life in some form or fashion; no one is immune from suffering. But rather than view the pain as our burden to bear, what if we considered it a gift for growing? Healing on the other side of heartbreak is not simply returning to how we were before the rending, but becoming better than we would have been without it—someone stronger, someone wiser, someone gentler.

Patricia is one of my heroes. For twenty-three years, she demonstrated total trust in God. She kept moving forward, regardless of how her husband tried to hold her back. And all these years later, she prays for Rodney still. His story is not over.

Today, Patricia is remarried to a wonderful man who loves and cherishes her like I had always hoped someone would. Her three grown children are all married and love Jesus. When I watch her laughing and playing with her grandchildren, I'm always amazed that the joy I see in her now is no different than the joy I saw during her dark chapters. She's a light. Always has been.

How did she do it? How does she do it now? She focuses on what Jesus has done for her rather than on what people haven't. And she's grateful. Struggles help remove the fluff of our faith to make it rock solid. Patricia's story taught her the truth of that. Growth and gratitude are the lens through which she views her story. Perspective makes all the difference in how we interpret the narrative and how we summarize the facts.

Patricia is now in her sixties. From time to time a young wife will come to her for counsel about marriage struggles. She opens her Bible and says, "Let me tell you a story." Some don't like what she has to say; some do.

> *Struggles help remove the fluff of our faith to make it rock solid.*

Patricia is not bitter or resentful of those twenty-three years. She doesn't see them as wasted but invested. "I have no regrets," she says, smiling. "Only blessings. The three greatest being my children, whom I would have never had without him."

These aren't the words of a Bible teacher or seminary graduate. They are the words of a woman who trusted God through the darkest chapters of her life and continues to trust him through the happiest ones today. She lives loved every day. Clings to every word in the Bible. Believes them. Breathes them. Battles with them. As I tell her often, I want to be like her when I grow up.

LOOKING THROUGH THE RIGHT LENS

Are there some parts of your story that you would like to rewrite? I'm sure there are. We all have them. But here's another way to think of it—are there maybe some parts of your story you just need to reread through a different lens?

If you've ever had an eye exam for glasses, you're familiar with the refraction test the doctor uses to determine what prescription is right for you. You place your face up to a Phoroptor (I had to look that up. Who knew?), and then the doctor flips down first one lens, then another, while you say which of the two helps you see the letters on the wall more clearly. Lens one or lens two? Lens three or lens four? Which one is better? And so it goes. Could it be that we are looking at our stories through the wrong lens, and if we would simply flip down a different one, we would see a better story? I wonder.

Maybe where we see trials, God sees training. Where we see struggle, God sees strength-building. Where we see a failure, God sees a future. Where we see problems, God sees promises. Where we see probable defeat, God sees ultimate victory. Where we see past pain, God sees the best is yet to come. Which lens is clearer? Lens one or lens two?

The apostle Paul was a man whose physical eyesight waned with the passing years, but his spiritual eyesight remained exceptionally clear. During his time of preaching the gospel, he had been flogged, whipped, and stoned many times. He had been shipwrecked, snake-bitten, outcast, and ridiculed. Several times, he was in lockdown in one place or another. Part of the time he was under house arrest in Rome; part of the time he was in a dirty dungeon chained to a guard—all for preaching the gospel. And yet, it was during one of those stints in prison that Paul wrote the most joyful book in the New Testament: Philippians.

I want you to know, brothers and sisters, that what has happened to me has actually served to advance the gospel. As a result, it has become clear throughout the whole palace guard and to everyone else that I am in chains for Christ. And because of my chains, most of the brothers and sisters have become confident in the Lord and dare all the more to proclaim the gospel without fear. (Philippians 1:12–14)

Lens one or lens two? Paul didn't see himself as stuck in prison *because* of Jesus; he saw himself as stationed in prison *for* Jesus. He didn't see himself as chained to a Roman guard; he saw the Roman guard as chained to him. The guards had to listen to Paul talk about Jesus day in and day out. Paul had time to write letters to all the churches, something he might not have been able to do had he continued to travel from place to place.

Just because something takes our lives in an unexpected direction doesn't mean that God had a hiccup in his master plan. Paul said that what happened to him had served to advance the gospel. In other words, *It's not about me. It's about the gospel. I am in chains because of the gospel. Not as a result of the gospel but in order to advance the gospel.*

Paul also wrote, "I am *put here* for the defense of the gospel" (v. 16, emphasis added). Who put him there? From the outside looking in, it appeared the Roman rulers put him there. But from the inside looking out, Paul knew God had positioned him there. He didn't see himself as stuck at all. He considered himself stationed.

Paul was a master of lens-flipping. "We are hard pressed on every side, but not crushed," he wrote, "perplexed, but not in despair; persecuted, but not abandoned; struck down, but not destroyed" (2 Corinthians 4:8–9). Can't you just see the lens flipping back and forth? Lens one or lens two? Which helps you see the situation more clearly?

Pastor Steven Furtick once said about Paul's prison perspective that, regardless of how he got there, he understood that he was put there. "That's a way of seeing life that will set you free . . . to decide in advance, wherever I end up, that must be where God has me. . . . When the situation is out of my control, it's not out of God's hands."[1]

Even though Paul was seemingly stuck in a cycle of one bad thing happening after another, he still had joy. I'm sure he wasn't happy all the time, but he was still joyful. There's a big difference. Joy can be a happy feeling, but it's also more than that. It's a point of view. The Bible says this about Jesus: "For the joy set before him he endured the cross" (Hebrews 12:2). I don't think Jesus was happy about going to the cross, but I do think he was joyful in the suffering.

Joy isn't the absence of sadness. We can't choose our feelings in a bad story, but we can choose our focus. We can choose to trust that God is a good God even on a bad day. Even though we may not be able to fix our problems, we can fix our focus on Jesus, the author and perfecter of our faith, who can fix our problems.

I wish I could tell you that I have this perspective all the time. I don't. It's a struggle. I pout. I get huffy. I get downright discouraged when my plans fall apart or people don't respond the way I'd hoped. But after I settle down, I try to remember to flip the lens and look at my circumstances through the sovereignty of God rather than the selfishness of Sharon. And then I have a better story. Not because the storyline changes, but because I read it differently.

When we flip the lens and read our stories through God's sovereign truth and unfailing love, we might realize that we have titled our stories, or at least a few chapters, incorrectly. Think about the titles you have put on some of your darkest chapters. Write them down. Go ahead, I'll wait.

Now go back and consider those chapters through the lens of God's sovereign truth and unfailing love. Do you need to change a few of those chapter titles? I'll admit, that's exactly what I had to do. Let me give you one example.

STANDING IN THE DOORWAY
OF A DIFFERENT STORY

When I experienced God's no to my desire to have a houseful of children, the devil was right there. He taunted, *God doesn't love you. If God loved you, your baby wouldn't have died. He'd bless you with more children. Those Bible verses work for other people, but they don't work for you. Who are you kidding?*

For a time, those lies were the lens I looked through to interpret my story. However, it was the wrong lens. Several years later, I was standing in the doorway of Steven's room, looking at him while he slept. He was a sixteen-year-old tangle of sheets and limbs. He was now six feet long, needed a shave, and sported a mass of shaggy brown hair. Drool slid down his slack-jawed face. I stood there thinking, *Man, I love this kid.*

Suddenly, God's Word washed over me.

For God so loved the world that he gave his one and only Son, that whoever believes in him shall not perish but have eternal life.

"Is that you, Lord?" I whispered.

For God so loved the world that he gave his one and only Son, that whoever believes in him shall not perish but have eternal life.

There I stood, frozen in the doorway, staring at my . . . only son. I had known that Bible verse long before I knew Jesus. However, until that moment, I had never understood the weighty worth of the words so fully. See, I have an *only son.* I love many people in this world, but there is no one I love enough to sacrifice my only son. And yet, God loved me and you enough to sacrifice his.

I flipped the lens that day. I no longer viewed my story through the lens of the lie that God didn't love me, but the lens of just how much he did. God had given me a living, breathing, walking, talking example of the depth and breadth of his love. Every time I look at that grown man-child, I'm reminded of God's great sacrifice—giving his *only Son* for me and for you.

Lens one or lens two? Which one is better? The lens of God's perfect love will always give us a clearer perspective. It is through that lens that we can give our stories a better title.

Chapter Twelve

The Perfect Ending to an Imperfect Story

Our broken lives are not lost or useless. God's love is still
working. He comes in and takes the calamity and uses
it victoriously, working out his wonderful plan of love.

—Eric Liddel, *Disciplines of the Christian Life*

I looped my hand through the crook of Steven's arm. Music filled the room. Family and friends turned in their seats. Grins just about cracked our faces. Steven walked me down the aisle and kissed my cheek. I kissed him back. Then I took my seat on the front row, first chair on the right—the mother of the groom. Steven and Emily's wedding day was a joy-filled day with God's presence spilling over the celebration.

Tears filled my eyes as I watched and listened to the couple say their vows, but not just the normal "I'm so proud of my son and tickled that he's marrying this wonderful girl" sort of tears. These were tears because of what God had done in the past fifteen years to get us to this place. You see, my son was that young man I mentioned in chapter 1, the one who was beating my socks off at Gin Rummy, the one who

187

felt life was too hard to keep living during his junior year of college. Steven's phone call the day after he was rushed to the hospital was the opening page to the worst chapter of my life. Every single page of what you've just read in this book has been filtered through the tears, trauma, and triumph of that experience. Questions. Forgiveness. Shame. Healing. Fear. And, oh yes, resurrection.

The word *denouement* (day-noo-MON) is a French word that describes the part of a story or a movie in which all the questions are answered, the problems are solved, or the outcome of a complex sequence of events are explained. The word literally means "to untie." A writer of a good story will give you bits of information about the plot throughout, but save the most stunning revelations for the end, rewarding readers for staying the course. And I've found that God often does the same. There are some questions we may not have answered, problems we may not have solved, or outcomes that may not be explained until the end. But I can assure you, God is the masterful writer. No one can write a story like he can. In the end, God will tie up the loose ends and undo the tangled knots. One day, your story will all make sense.

I don't know what you've gone through or what you're going through right now, but I do know this. God is not finished writing your story. Don't give up on your story because the chapter you're in right now is hard. Keep moving forward. Take the next step. And then the next. God has the power to forgive the unforgiveable, to mend the unrepairable, to redeem the unredeemable, and to get you through the worst chapters imaginable. And not just get you through them, but make you better for it.

The Bible opens with the words "In the beginning." In the beginning, the earth was formless and empty, darkness was over the surface of the deep, and the Spirit of God was hovering over the waters. And then God spoke, and what was not became what is. As he spoke the world into existence, he wrote your story into the narrative. And he's still writing your story even now.

There's more to be written—more life to be lived, more miracles to experience, more chains to break, more steps to take. Embrace the story God has given you. Even the parts where you grabbed the pen from his hand and tried to write on your own. Even the parts where someone else burst in uninvited and created chaos. The scenes we'd rather skip can become the redemptive highlights of God's glory.

Give your story a new title if you'd like. One that reflects the epilogue you never saw coming. The Romans 8:28 of it all—how God is working in all things for your good.

THE PERFECT ENDING

After both my parents came to Christ, my family's storyline took a dramatic turn. It wasn't a sharp turn but a gradual curve. It wasn't easy, but it was good. However, not everyone in the narrative was willing to release the broken shards. Some chose to cling to bitterness and grasped resentment with a tight, unrelenting fist, as if saying, "No way will I ever let this go. I'll hang on to my hate." Those were the ones who stayed stuck in a bad story rather than moving ahead into a new one. But even now, I know the pen is still in God's hand.

Everybody wants a new beginning, but what about a new ending? Do you believe you can write a new ending to your story? That you can take that period at the end of a chapter and add two more dots to it? Those three dots . . . are called an ellipsis. They mean "to be continued." No author writes "The End" at the end of a single chapter. Your story isn't over until God says it's over and calls you home. Don't get stuck in a chapter when God is inviting you to simply turn the page. I'm so glad I was with my mom when she turned the page to the end of her story.

I sat with her as the last six weeks of her final chapter were being written. She was dying and we knew it. Mom told the doctors to unhook the machines and stop the fluid drips that were keeping her alive. "I'm ready to go," she said. "I'm not afraid."

With tears in my eyes I said, "Well, Mom, it looks like you're going to get to see Jesus before me."

With a mischievous twinkle in her eye she said, "Are you jealous?" For a minute, I was.

We had such a fun time those last six weeks. We laughed at funny stories and cried about a few. She bossed me around from her hospital bed, just like she'd done my entire life. "Don't forget to use lip liner," she scolded, as if it were the most important thing on earth. "And your hair, you really need to use this product I've been using. It's under my bathroom sink at home. I think it could help you with your lack of shine problem." (I never knew I had a lack of shine problem.) But rather than get ticked off, I got tickled. It just didn't bother me so much anymore.

"Really, Mom? Those are your parting words of wisdom?"

"Well, what else have we got to talk about?"

One afternoon, she was propped up in her hospital bed and I caught her gazing out the window. "Whatcha' thinking about, Momma?" I asked.

"I'm thinking, it's not how you start but how you finish."

"Who told you that?" I asked.

"You did," she replied.

She finished well.

And, friend, that's what I want to leave you with. It's not how you start but how you finish. I'm not talking about how you finish your last days on this earth. I'm talking about how you finish today—and tomorrow, and each day that follows. How you finish each chapter God is writing of your story as it blends into his.

Momma died a few days after our conversation about finishing well. Sure, she had dark chapters all throughout her life, many of them with my name written in the narrative. But we both handed those shards of a busted life to the Potter who mended the cracks with the gold and silver veins of grace. All I can say is, it was stunning.

It was the end of a chapter for me, but for Mom, it was the beginning of forever.

THE PARADOX OF A GOOD STORY

It's a paradox that the worst chapters can become our greatest victories, but isn't that the way of Scripture?

Jesus died like a criminal and now rules as a king.

God temporarily blinded Saul physically so that he could see spiritually.

Paul was chained to a guard to learn how to live free.

I die to self in order to live for God.

What I considered the most pitiful parts of my story I now consider the most powerful.

Joni Eareckson Tada, a woman who was paralyzed from the neck down after a tragic dive into shallow water, offers a beautiful perspective on what it means to trust God with the paradoxes in our stories.

> God may design some chapters in our lives to be long and delightful; others, far too short, and sometimes painful. But we only see the meaning of our story when it fits into the context of a bigger, far greater story of Jesus Christ himself. My best life-chapters were not the easy, breezy days of being on my feet; they were the deep ones when I was suffering and groping for the arms of my Savior. . . . When it comes to happy endings, you can't find a better Author than the God of the Bible.[1]

Will you trust God to write your story? Even when you feel he's surely dropped the pen and walked away, will you trust that he hasn't?

Even when you feel that he's made a mistake in the writing, will you trust that his plan is still intact? Even when the story seems anything but good, will you trust that he is good? A good ending is more than the resolution to a conflict. A good ending is one of redemption.

When it comes to the worst chapters of your past, whether it was your fault, or you had no choice in its unfolding, you can't change it. I can't change mine either. We can only change what we do with it. We can bury the worst chapters in secret graves of shame, bitterness, and fear, or plant the seeds of what we've learned into the hearts and lives of others.

Hardships often prepare ordinary people for an extraordinary destiny. I believe that for you. I know a name that is greater than your pain. I know a name that is greater than your shame. And that name is Jesus—the *author* and perfecter of our faith.

God rarely writes tidy Hallmark stories that tie everything up with a neat shiny bow in ninety minutes or less.

Hardships often prepare ordinary people for an extraordinary destiny.

Most of the accounts in the Bible are convoluted and messy. And so are our lives. Each story in his transcendent story has characters, plot twists, tragedy, resolution, redemption, and ultimately a conclusion. In his ultimate story—in which we get to play a part—the end has already been written. The ultimate denouement.

Then I saw "a new heaven and a new earth," for the first heaven and the first earth had passed away, and there was no longer any sea. I saw the Holy City, the new Jerusalem, coming down out of heaven from God, prepared as a bride beautifully dressed for her husband. And I heard a loud voice from the throne saying, "Look! God's dwelling place is now among the people, and he will dwell with them. They will be his people, and God himself will be with them and be their God. 'He will wipe every tear from their eyes.

There will be no more death' or mourning or crying or pain, for the old order of things has passed away."

He who was seated on the throne said, "I am making everything new!" Then he said, "Write this down, for these words are trustworthy and true." (Revelation 21:1–5)

Until you cross over from this life into the next, the pen is still in God's hand. The amazing thing is that God allows us to participate in the writing. He gives us choices; we make decisions. Tragedy beats us down; he raises us up again. Each storyline is meant to be one of victorious celebration as we are refined like gold.

I believe with the psalmist, "All my days were written in your book and planned before a single one of them began" (Psalm 139:16 csb). I don't know where you are today or how you feel about the chapter you're in, but from where I sit, I can honestly say, I love my story.

God changes
graves into gardens
mourning into dancing
ashes into beauty
seaways into highways
rivers into roadways
dry bones into armies
shame into glory
a cross into a crown
our worst chapters into our greatest victories.

Acknowledgments

Without hundreds of men and women sharing their stories with me through the years, this book would never had come to be. I am so grateful that they trusted me with some of their worst chapters that God has used for His best purposes.

This being my twenty-fifth book brings up a deep well of gratitude for the people who have traveled this journey with me. Thank you to Nancy Young who pulled out a Proverbs 31 Homemaker Newsletter from under her car seat in 1985 and said, "Maybe you should contact them?" And then there was Lysa TerKeurst, a young momma writing about cheerios stuck to the floor and crayon scribbles on the wall, who said, "Let's do this together." Gayle Roper from CLASS who told me the difference between someone who writes and a published author is that the published author doesn't give up. She was right.

I am so grateful for the decade of pouring into the genesis of Proverbs 31 Ministries and watching it move from a simple newsletter for homemakers to a worldwide ministry that seeks to eradicate biblical poverty. I learned way more from the process than I contributed.

My heart swells thinking of Glynnis Whitwer who joined P31 in 1998 and remains one of my biggest cheerleaders and closest friends today. Her encouragement kept me tethered to P31 after I passed the baton of leadership to run a different course and welcomed me back when the race merged paths one again.

Bill Jensen has been invaluable to me as an agent and a friend. With warmth and wisdom, Bill has been a brainstorming, idea-bouncing, door-knocking, heart-checking encourager who has pointed me to roads previously not taken and then helped me get there. He's an original renaissance man who can fight off a bear in the woods while listening to the opera *Falstaff* through his earbuds.

Gwen Smith and Mary Southerland, my precious, much loved Girlfriends in God, have kept me consistently moving forward for the past fifteen years. What would I do without them? I hope I never have to find out. We could not be more different in gifting and personality and yet more similar in our passion and calling.

I am so grateful for the Thomas Nelson team: Jessica Wong who wielded her amazing editing skills to made the book stronger, Janene MacIvor who sanded the rough edges to make it smoother, and Karen Jackson who mapped out the marketing plan to have maximum reach.

There are so many people who have been part of this ministry journey: Alan Watts, Dan Simeone, Brooke Martinez, Angela Bouma, Jill Archer, Karen Shiels, Kim Abe, Pat Layton, Carol Kent, Pam Farrell, Rachel Wojo, Julie Gillies, Jill Savage, the Proverbs 31 staff, just to name a few.

My husband, Steve, has been the one person who has believed in me and encouraged me more than any other. He continues to think me more capable than I really am and love me more than I deserve. My son, Steven, who has been the main character of many of my life-changing stories, has stretched the boundaries of my small thinking, strengthened the resolve of my flimsy feelings, and helped me see the world through a different lens than I would have without him. I love both of these two Steves more than life.

I am humbled and honored that God has allowed me to traverse this path of words on the page. It is only through the finished work of Jesus Christ on the cross and His Spirit in me that the worst chapters of my life have become my greatest victories. To God be the glory.

My True Identity in Christ

Matthew

I am the salt of the earth. (5:13)
I am the light of the world. (5:14)
I am valuable to God. (6:26)

John

I am indwelled by Christ. His Spirit lives in me. (14:20)
I am a branch of the True Vine. (15:5)
I am Christ's friend. (15:15)
I am chosen and appointed by Christ to go and bear fruit. (15:16)

Romans

I am justified by Christ's blood. (5:9)
I am reconciled to God through Christ's death and saved through
    Christ's life. (5:10)
I am set free from sin and a slave of righteousness. (6:18)
I am free from condemnation. (8:1)
I am free in Christ. (8:2)
I am a child of God and a co-heir with Christ. (8:17)
I am more than a conqueror through Christ. (8:37)
I am accepted by Christ. (15:7)

1 Corinthians

I have the mind of Christ. (2:16)

I am a temple of God. His Spirit lives in me. (3:16)

I am washed, sanctified, and justified through Christ. (6:11)

I am a temple of the Holy Spirit. (6:19)

I am part of Christ's body. (12:27)

2 Corinthians

I am the fragrance of Christ. (2:15)

I am a new creation. (5:17)

I am an ambassador for Christ and a minister of reconciliation. (5:20)

I am righteous in Christ. (5:21)

Galatians

I am redeemed from the curse of the law. (3:13)

I am a child of God and an heir of God. (4:7)

Ephesians

I am a saint, one of God's holy people. (1:1)

I am blessed with every spiritual blessing in Christ. (1:3)

I am adopted into God's family. (1:5)

I am redeemed and forgiven through Christ's blood. (1:7)

I am chosen by God. (1:11)

I am sealed by God with the Holy Spirit. (1:13)

I am now alive with Christ. (2:5)

I am God's handiwork created in Christ Jesus to do good works which God prepared in advance for me to do. (2:10)

I am a fellow citizen with God's people and a member of God's household. (2:19)

Philippians
I am a citizen of heaven. (3:20)
I am able to do all things through Christ who gives
    me strength. (4:13)

Colossians
I am rescued from the dominion of darkness and brought
    into the kingdom of God's Son. (1:13)
I am holy in God's sight, without blemish and free
    of accusation. (1:22)
I am complete in Christ. (2:10 NASB)
I am hidden with Christ in God. (3:3)
I am chosen by God, holy, and dearly loved. (3:12)

1 Peter
I am of a chosen people, a royal priesthood, a holy nation,
    a people belonging to God to declare the praises of him
    who called me out of darkness into his wonderful light. (2:9)
I am a foreigner and exile in this world. (2:11)
I am an enemy of the devil. (5:8)

1 John
I am forgiven of my sins. (1:9)
I am a child of God. (3:1–2)
I am born of God and the evil one (the devil) cannot
    harm me. (5:18)

Revelation
I am the bride of Christ. (21:9)

Prayer for Forgiving Others

Heavenly Father,

Today I am making a decision to forgive as you have forgiven me. I admit that I have been carrying resentment, anger, and bitterness as a weight. Today, I release that weight and place it on your shoulders. I forgive _____ for _____. I will no longer be held captive by unforgiveness but will live free. I will no longer hold the offense against the offender but place _____ in your hands. I will no longer rehearse the offense in my mind but will repeat your grace in my heart. I realize that I cannot do this on my own and acknowledge the power of the Holy Spirit who enables me to do all you have called me to do. And when I feel a trigger of remembrance, help me to acknowledge anew that I have put the offense behind me and forgiven the offender. It is finished.

In Jesus' name,

Amen

Prayer for Receiving
God's Forgiveness

Heavenly Father,

I come to you now and ask that you forgive me for _____.
I thank you that your Word says that if we confess our sins to you, you are faithful and just to forgive us and cleanse us from all unrighteousness. Thank you that your Word is true and that you have wiped my slate clean and thrown my sins into the deepest of seas to remember them no more. Thank you that there is now no condemnation for those who are in Christ Jesus. Today, I receive your forgiveness, and thus forgive myself. I will not believe the lies of the enemy that try to make me believe I am still guilty and shameful. I choose to believe the truth that I am forgiven and free of condemnation. Thank you that the blood of Jesus covers my past mistakes, sins, and failures. Today I walk out from under the cloud of shame and into the light of Christ. I release the burden of guilt and leave it at the foot of the cross. It is finished.

In Jesus' name,

Amen

BIBLE STUDY GUIDE

One of the difficulties in writing a book is that one has to pick and choose which biblical truths to include. However, God has so much more to say about the importance of our stories. This study guide is for those who want to dig deeper into God's Word and unearth even more of his glorious treasures regarding the importance of our stories. Each lesson will expand on the themes of the coinciding chapters, while taking us further into the Scripture.

I would recommend reading the chapter first so you have a foundation for the teaching before going through the corresponding lesson. If you are doing this with a small group, consider having one group member share her story each week. Perhaps, as you draw near to the end of the study, plan a craft day together where you can use broken china or glass to create a beautiful mosaic.

You'll notice that there is no space to write your comments or answers. I suggest using a separate journal or notebook to record your answers.

I pray that God will open the eyes of your heart through this study to experience the depth, breadth, and heights of his great love and purpose for you.

Lesson 1

May I Please Have a
Different Story?

As I mentioned in chapter 1, everyone loves a good story. Let's take some time this week to consider some of your favorites.

1. What was your favorite childhood story or fairytale? Who were the main characters? The villain? The hero? What was the plot twist that made the story interesting? What was the overall conflict in the story? How was the conflict resolved? Do you see any parallels to how your life story has played out?

2. Our lives come equipped with all the elements necessary for a good story: setting, characters, plot, conflict, and resolution or redemption. There is drama, adventure, romance, mystery, protagonists, and antagonists. Can you think of one story in your life that includes some of these key elements? If so, jot down what each element was in your story.

3. Write down the "titles" of three of the most difficult and most delightful chapters of your story. Note the elements of story from above. Share the titles with a friend or with your group if you feel comfortable.

4. What do you hope to take away from this study of *When You Don't Like Your Story*?

Lesson 2

Why Me? Why This? Why Now?

In chapter 2, we looked at several reasons as to why bad things happen. In today's lesson, let's delve into another story that shows how what looks like a bad story can turn into a great story.

1. Read John 11 all the way through. Then take a closer look at verse 6: "So when he heard that Lazarus was sick, he stayed where he was two more days." The sentence doesn't say, *but* Jesus stayed there two more days, as if it were a careless mistake. It says *so,* as if it were a calculated plan. Because it was. What questions does the word *so* stir in your heart?

2. Many Christians think that if we do A and B, then God will do C. But that's often not the case, and it certainly wasn't how things happened with Lazarus's sickness. Why was Jesus glad that he wasn't there to heal Lazarus? Why would God be glad that something that feels like it is tearing us apart has happened?

3. The name Lazarus means "the one who God helps." How did Martha and Mary respond to Jesus' lack of help (vv. 21, 32)?

4. Notice how Martha self-corrected her response to Jesus' question when he arrived. What did she say in verse 22?

5. Read Matthew 8:5–13. Did Jesus need to be present to heal Lazarus? Can you think of other instances in Scripture where we see the far reach of God's power?

6. Read John 11:38–57 and note what happens once Jesus arrives at Lazarus's tomb. Who was present? What was the outcome for Lazarus, the onlookers, the religious leaders, Jesus, and his disciples?

7. Fill in the blanks of this sentence: If Jesus had healed Lazarus, it would have been a _____ story. Because Jesus raised Lazarus from the dead, it was a _____ story.

8. Matthew, Mark, and Luke are called the Synoptic Gospels, meaning they record similar stories and sequence of events. John wrote the story of Jesus to show who Jesus was, so some details are out of sequence in his account. John wrote the story of Jesus to show who Jesus was, so some details are out of order in his account. What does John tell us about Mary in chapter 11 that doesn't happen until chapter 12 (11:2; 12:1–8)? In the US, we sometimes use the term "Chapter 11" in reference to when someone files for bankruptcy. Here's our challenge for today: Can we believe that the chapter 12 of praise is on the way even when we feel we're in the spiritually bankrupt chapter 11 of life? Give an example.

9. Write down a difficult situation you are in today and how you truly feel about it. Then add, "Even now I know . . ." to the end of that story. Write down what you know to be true even though you can't see it with your eyes right now. End today's lesson with a prayer including the words "even now I know."

Lesson 3

There's Always a Meanwhile

In chapter 3 we saw that God is always working; there is always a "meanwhile" that we can't see. Let's put some puzzle pieces together to discover God's meanwhile that reached from Hannah to King David.

1. Read 1 Samuel 1:1–20 and describe Hannah's situation. Then skip over to 1 Samuel 2:12–36. What was the situation with the priests, namely Eli and his sons, at the same time Hannah was praying for a child?

2. Now, flip back over to 1 Samuel 2:21–28. If you're using the NIV, NKJV, or NLT, note the word *meanwhile* in verse 21. After years of infertility, how did God bless Hannah, and what did she do with this blessing? Hannah wanted a son; God needed a prophet. How did God work in Hannah's and Samuel's meanwhile to raise up a prophet that would change the course of Israel's history? Once the prophet was born, how did God continue to bless Hannah (2:21)?

3. Read 1 Samuel 2:1–10. List all the words of triumph in Hannah's prayer.

4. For those whose mother's heart breaks at the thought of

Hannah relinquishing her son to Eli's care, read 1 Samuel 7:17 and note where Samuel visited often as an adult.

5. Let's fast-forward. Read 1 Samuel 16. What did God call Samuel to do in verse 1? Write down what you learn about the boy David. Where was David when Samuel asked to see Jesse's sons? What does the fact that Jesse didn't call David in from the fields when Samuel asked to see his sons say about what he thought of David?

6. Read 1 Samuel 16:14–23. Where did David go after he was anointed as Israel's next king (v. 19)? Did he wear a crown and take his seat on the throne? Why do you think that was the case?

7. Sometime later, David's preparation met God's invitation. Read 1 Samuel 17. How had God been working in David's meanwhile to prepare him for this moment (vv. 34–37)?

8. Now for the part your Sunday school teacher left out. What did David use to cut off Goliath's head (1 Samuel 17:51)? What two things did David take away from the battle (1 Samuel 17:53–54)?

9. Now fast-forward several years. After David killed Goliath, King Saul grew very jealous and sought to kill him for many years. In 1 Samuel 21, David is trapped in the town of Nob without a weapon. At the right place, at the right time, what did God provide for David (vv. 1–9)? How was God working behind the scenes to make sure that David had what he needed when he needed it?

10. Theologian A. B. Simpson said, "God is preparing his heroes; and when the opportunity comes, he can fit them into their places in a moment, and the world will wonder where they

came from." What do John 5:17 and Psalm 121:1–5 tell us about God working even when we can't see it or feel it?

11. Consider praying Hannah's prayer from 1 Samuel 2:1–10 in the midst of your meanwhile situation.

Lesson 4

The Scab You Won't Stop Picking

In chapter 4, the big question is, *Do you want to get well?* Do you want to stop picking at the scab and allow healing to happen? The Israelites were faced with the same dilemma. Did they want to take hold of the unknown of the promised land or stay stuck in the familiarity of the bondage of Egypt? Let's take a closer look together.

1. Read Genesis 45. How did the Israelites end up in Egypt (vv. 16–20)? What happened between the time of Joseph and the time of Exodus 1? Describe their plight.

2. Read Exodus 2. What did Moses do (vv. 11–15)? Did God call him to do this? What was the result?

3. From Moses' call in Exodus 3 to the day he led the Israelites out of Egypt and across the wilderness, he performed many miracles. When it came time for them to march into the land God had promised, Moses sent in twelve spies. Read Numbers 13 and 14. Describe the unbelieving report of the ten spies (13:26–29, 31–33) and the believing report of the two spies (13:30; 14:7–9). Who did the people believe? Where did they want to go back to and why (14:3–4)? What was the end result

of their refusal to believe God and take hold of what he had already promised (14:20–25)?

4. How is what happened with the people of Israel similar to a Christian who is free from the penalty of sin but refusing to take hold of the promises of God? Can a person be saved from the penalty of sin but wander in the wilderness of unbelief? Explain.

5. Now fast-forward thirty-eight years or so, and read Joshua 1. What did God remind Joshua? What did Joshua remind the people? How many spies did Joshua send into Jericho (Joshua 2:1)? How does that compare with the number Moses sent in?

6. Read Joshua 2:8–11 and Joshua 6:1. Why were the gates of Jericho shut up so tightly? Note how Rahab mentions God parting the Red Sea and not the Jordan River. How does the truth of the Jericho people's fear of the Israelites compare with the ten spies' report in Numbers 13:31–33?

7. Read Joshua 6:3–5. What was God's battle plan? Even though the Lord had already given them the city, what did the people of Israel have to do (Joshua 1:3; 6:3–5)?

8. Think of a memory that has built a wall around your heart. God wants you to live free and take the territory that he has already declared to be yours. But you have a choice between being generation 1 or generation 2. Read Philippians 3:12–14. What does God require of us for the walls to come down in our own lives?

9. We are just starting this journey, so don't get frustrated if this lesson is still too hard to grasp completely. We'll come back to it again. For now, read and record Philippians 1:4–6. Put it on a card in a prominent place to remind yourself of the journey and the One doing the work.

Lesson 5

Changing the Ending to Your Story

Chapter 5 was a big step—a high step—toward having a better story. Let's dig a little deeper into the truths of forgiveness in order to make them a reality in our lives.

1. Read Hebrews 12:15, Ephesians 4:26–27, and 2 Corinthians 2:10–11. Unforgiveness makes us a slow-moving target for the enemy. What can happen to our hearts when we choose not to forgive?

2. Read Romans 12:17–21. What does the Bible teach us about exacting revenge for the wrong done to us?

3. Read Matthew 6:12–15; 18:21–35; and Luke 6:37. What did Jesus teach about forgiving others in these verses?

4. Read Colossians 3:13. What did Paul teach about forgiving others? Explain what that looks like.

5. While reading chapter 5 of this book, did God put a finger on any possible manifestations of bitterness in your life—emotional, physical, mental? Some examples might include holding grudges, withholding compliments or encouragement, jealousy, anger, negativity, ingratitude, being judgmental, or argumentativeness.

6. Record Jesus' words on the cross found in Luke 23:34. Now read Psalm 22:6–7 and Isaiah 53:3. How were the people who crucified Jesus described? Did Jesus wait for an apology before he forgave those who were torturing him?

7. Is there someone from whom you are still waiting for an apology before you forgive him or her? If so, what do we learn from Jesus' example on the cross?

8. Read John 13:15. What did Jesus tell us we should do with the example he has set? How did Stephen follow Jesus' example in Acts 7:54–60? How can we do the same?

9. When you choose to forgive, you move from being the victim in your story to the victor with Jesus as your hero. Ponder that sentence and note where you are in the process.

10. Did God reveal anyone that you need to forgive? An offense you've been carrying around that needs to be released once and for all? If so, turn to the Prayer for Forgiving Others on page 200, and live free.

Lesson 6

Leaving the Shame Place

God never intended for any of his children to live in the shame place. In this lesson we will look at a woman who went there and stayed there, and about a king who gave his life so we don't have to.

1. Read 2 Samuel 13:1–22. Record the main characters in the story and who they were in relation to David and each other. Since Tamar is a king's daughter, what does that make her? What else do you learn about her in those first verses? Her character? Her standing? Her appearance? Her trust in others?

2. Summarize what happened to Tamar.

3. What do we learn about the importance of crying out about this sort of crime from Deuteronomy 22:23–27? What was Tamar's response to the rape (2 Samuel 13:18–19)? Tearing clothes, putting on sackcloth, and covering the head in ashes were all signs of mourning and grief in the Bible. (See Genesis 37:34–35; Joshua 7:1–9; and 2 Samuel 12:15–17.) In that culture, people didn't have many clothes and the ones they did have were costly. What was the significance of Tamar's robe, and what did tearing it signify?

4. What did Absalom tell Tamar to do? How does this relate to what we learned about shame in chapter 6?

5. What was David's reaction to Amnon's actions (2 Samuel 13:21)? What did he do about it? Now read 2 Samuel 13:23–34. How did Absalom avenge Tamar two years later? Who should have been the one to take control of the situation and punish Amnon?

6. Perhaps one of the saddest lines in this passage is verse 20: "And Tamar lived in her brother Absalom's house, a desolate woman." Even though her perpetrator was dead, she remained in her pain and suffering. Define the word *desolate*.

7. Tamar's earthly father was not there for her, and maybe yours wasn't either. But your heavenly Father is . . . and so is his Son, King Jesus. Read the following verses and look at what God the Father and God the Son did to remove your shame: Isaiah 50:7; Isaiah 53:1–10; John 3:16; Romans 10:9–11; Hebrews 12:1–3; and 1 Peter 2:6. In despair, Tamar cried out, "Where could I carry my shame?" (see 2 Samuel 13:13 ESV). Friend, where will you carry yours?

8. After the abuse, was Tamar still a princess? Was she living like a princess? Why or why not?

9. Whether it's a traumatic event at the hands of another or the results from our own poor choices, God never intends for us to be stuck in the sackcloth and ashes of desolation. How is staying in a shame place ignoring or minimalizing what Jesus has done for you? How does staying in the shame place keep you stuck in a bad story?

10. If you could have visited Tamar during her time of desolation, what would you have said to her? Now, what do you need to say to yourself?

Lesson 7

When Forgetting Is Not Enough

In our last lesson we spent some time with Tamar, urging her to come out of the shame place. I'm sure that if you could have, you would have encouraged her to put the crown back on her head. There *was* someone else who could have done that but didn't. Let's look at the difference he could have made if he had shared his story.

1. Do a quick review of the previous lesson. Now read 2 Samuel 11. Summarize the details of the story with the main characters, the plot, the problem, and the setting. List the sins that David committed.

2. What do we learn about the timing of this story in verse 1? Where should David have been (1 Samuel 8:20)?

3. Read 2 Samuel 12:1–25. Who sent Nathan to David? Summarize the scenario Nathan described and David's reaction to it. This is a wonderful example of the power of story. The way Nathan painted a story rather than pointed the finger allowed David to realize the weight of his guilt and pass judgment on himself. What did God say to David through Nathan (vv. 5–10)? Record David's response in verse 13.

4. Read Psalm 51, believed to have been written during the time of David's remorse. What does David say about his own personal sackcloth and ashes from his sin of sleeping with Bathsheba? What did David say he would do when God forgave him (v. 13)?

5. Read Psalm 31 and Psalm 103:1–12. What evidence do we have that God forgave David of his sin? How does this echo 1 John 1:9?

6. David's sin was removed as far as the east is from the west. So all was well . . . or was it? Now, let's go back to Tamar and Amnon. How are these two stories similar?

7. We have no indication that David told his boys about his sin with Bathsheba and the fallout of that sin. They would have been old enough to remember the rumors. But how could David telling his story to his boys possibly have averted the situation?

8. We have no indication that Bathsheba told her story to Tamar. Sure, it was a dark chapter, a humiliating chapter, a scandalous story, but how could Bathsheba telling her story to Tamar have helped her leave her place of desolation? What could she have said to her to blow those ashes away?

9. What did Jesus tell Peter in Luke 22:32? How does telling your story strengthen others?

10. I hope 2 Corinthians 1:3–5 has become stamped on your heart. As we end today, record that passage, putting a big circle around the words "so that." What is your "so that" God is calling you to share?

Lesson 8

Why Your Story Matters

In our last lesson, we saw how Nathan painted a story rather than pointed a finger at King David. You've got something better than a made-up story; you have a God-story . . . and it matters!

1. Read Acts 10:1–8, 22. What do you learn about Cornelius, this commander of more than one hundred men? Was he Jewish or a Gentile? Honorable or dishonorable? What had he been praying?

2. Read Acts 10:9–23. Describe Peter's vision. What was God showing Peter through the vision? How was God preparing Peter to minister to the Gentiles?

3. How is the story of Peter and Cornelius a "meanwhile" story? What was God doing simultaneously in both Peter's and Cornelius's lives?

4. What did Peter realize in verses 34–48?

5. Not everyone was accepting of Peter's new ministry to the Gentiles. Read Acts 11:1–3. How did the apostles and brothers in Judea respond?

6. What did Peter do in Acts 11:4–17 to assure them? I hope you answered, "He told his story." Write out verse 4. What was the result of Peter telling his story? How is this story a fulfillment of God's prophecy to Abram in Genesis 12:2–3?

7. Have you ever experienced someone's going from protest to praise because of your or someone else's story? If so, explain.

8. As we know, the Bible is one big story about God, often referred to as a "metanarrative." Each book of the Bible is a story within a story of creation, the fall, redemption, and consummation. Read John 20:30–31. Why did John write his gospel? Did John write his gospel because he had heard about it or because he had actually witnessed it? How was John's personal story part of God's larger story? How is your personal story part of God's larger story? How does that truth give your story great significance?

9. Look up and record what the following verses say about God's plan for you: Psalm 139:16, John 15:16, and Ephesians 2:10. End today's lesson by asking God to make you sensitive to who needs to hear your story.

Lesson 9

Speaking Up When You Tend to Clam Up

When sharing our stories, we aren't trying to win an argument, but inviting people into a relationship with God. That removes the pressure, doesn't it? Let's sit by the well and see how one woman who had clammed up became a woman who spoke up.

1. Read the story of a woman who had clammed up in John 4:1–42. Jesus didn't have to go to Samaria because of geography. In fact, the Jews did everything they could to avoid the Samaritans, often crossing the Jordan and traveling on the east side just to avoid them. So why did Jesus go to Samaria? How does John 5:19 shed light on his decision?

2. Why was the woman at Jacob's well during the heat of the day rather than in the cool of the morning or evening when the other townswomen went?

3. Briefly describe the conversation between Jesus and the woman. Who did Jesus tell her he was (4:26)? Note, this is the first time Jesus revealed his identity to any one person . . . and it was a woman.

4. Initially, who was the woman trying to avoid by coming to the well in the heat of the day? After her encounter with Jesus, to whom did she run to tell her story (4:28)?

5. Read John 4:27–38. What was the disciples' reaction to Jesus talking to a woman? What was Jesus' reaction to the woman running to evangelize her town? How did he use her actions as an object lesson?

6. What was the result of the woman telling her story to the townspeople (John 4:39–42)?

7. This was just the beginning of the evangelism in Samaria. Where did Jesus tell the disciples to tell their stories in Acts 1:8? Considering what we know about the Jewish history and their dislike for the Samaritans, what would this commission have meant to these Jewish Christians (Galatians 3:28)? Read Acts 8:1–14 and 15:3. How did God make sure that they went to this area that held a special place in his heart?

8. Ponder this paraphrase from 2 Samuel 22:25. "GOD rewrote the text of my life when I opened the book of my heart to his eyes" (THE MESSAGE). How did God rewrite the text of the Samaritan woman's life? How did he rewrite the text of your life?

9. In closing today, read Psalm 145 and note everything the writer tells us about sharing our stories. Consider using the words as a prayer of thanksgiving.

Lesson 10

Disqualified? Says Who?

In chapter 10 we looked at our tendencies to feel disqualified because of our past circumstances. Today, let's see where those feelings come from and how to deal with them.

1. How is the devil referred to in Revelation 12:7–12? How do we see him in that role in Job 1? Define the word *accuser*.

2. The devil accuses and attacks our minds (our conscience) to convince us to shut up and shut down. Make a list of common accusations the accuser uses against God's people, such as calling them incapable, inadequate, a disappointment to God, sinful, stupid, too far gone, unforgivable, and others. Now go back and circle any you have felt about yourself. How are those accusations lies of the enemy geared to get you to shut up and shut down?

3. Going back to the four steps listed in chapter 10, what truths can you use to fight the lies you just listed? If you need help, refer to "My True Identity in Christ" on page 197.

4. What does Hebrews 9:11–14 tell us the blood of Christ cleanses? Define the word *conscience*, and then put that definition into the verse.

5. How does 2 Corinthians 1:2–7, Luke 22:32, and the story of the Samaritan woman contradict the idea that our past struggles, sins, or abuses disqualify us from telling our story to glorify God?

6. Read 2 Corinthians 3:4–6 and Colossians 1:9–14. Who has qualified you and made you competent?

7. What does 1 Corinthians 1:26–31 tell us about the kind of people God uses? Where do you fit into that verse?

8. Some people feel disqualified because of what others have said about them. Read 1 Samuel 17:32–37. Have you ever felt, "But, God, I am just a _____"? Fill in that blank and share it with a friend or your small group. What do you think God would say to whatever you put in that blank? I love that David told Saul, "I went after it" (v. 35). What is God calling you to "go after" today?

9. Read and record Acts 4:13, one of my favorite verses. What qualified this bunch of uneducated men? What qualifies you?

10. As Warren Weirsbe once said, "You can never be too small for God to use—only too big." If someone thinks that he or she is qualified in their own right, steer clear. What do we learn from James 4:10 about humility? Fill in the blanks: Every person is simply a (2 Corinthians 4:7)_____ empowered, equipped by the (Ephesians 3:14–19) _____, and qualified by (Colossians 1:12) _____.

Lesson 11

Lens One or Lens Two?
Which Is Better?

We've all heard the phrase that someone is either a glass-half-full or a glass-half-empty person. That's a similar principle to what we considered in chapter 10. In this lesson, let's see how Paul decided to look through the lens of providence and praise rather than the lens of problems and self-pity, and how that made the difference in the way he interpreted his story.

1. Read Acts 21:27–36. What happened to Paul in Jerusalem? What did he tell the people in Acts 21:37–22:21?

2. Briefly describe what happened to him in Acts 22:22–26:32. How much time passed between his appearing before Felix and Festus, and where was Paul that entire time (24:27)?

3. During Paul's imprisonment in Jerusalem, he was able to speak before King Agrippa. Read Acts 26 and note what Paul told the king. What was Agrippa's reply and Paul's response (vv. 28–29)? Who is responsible for the *outcome* of our obedience?

4. Read Acts 27. Where was the ship full of prisoners headed, and what were the conditions (vv. 1–9a)? What was Paul's warning,

and how did the men respond (vv. 9b–12)? Was Paul worried when the northeaster arose (vv. 13–26)? Why or why not? What was the lens through which Paul was viewing the situation?

5. Read Acts 28. How were the men received by the people of Malta—a place they never planned on going?

6. People want to attach a reason to your misery. Let's see how that faulty reasoning can lead to faulty conclusions. What did the island people think about Paul after the snake bit him (v. 4)? What did the island people think about Paul when he did not die from the snake bite (v. 6)? What does this tell you about the way humans incorrectly interpret others' situations? How is that a warning for us as we interpret our own stories, as well as the stories of others?

7. How did Paul make the most of his time in the place he never intended to be (28:7)? He could have spent his time looking through the lens of discouragement but chose to look through the lens of divine appointment. What does this teach us about looking for opportunities to glorify God even in circumstances of our stories that mystify us?

8. Paul spent his last two to three years of life in prison. While there, he wrote letters to the Ephesians, the Philippians, the Colossians, and to Philemon. Skim those letters and note ten verses of victory. How was he able to write verses on freedom while in chains (Galatians 5:1)?

9. While in chains, he also wrote, "Rejoice in the Lord always. I will say it again: Rejoice!" (Philippians 4:4). We learn by putting into practice what we've put in our heads. Write out a declaration of how you will flip the lens of discouragement to a declaration of God's goodness (Philippians 4:9; 1 Timothy 4:15).

10. What is one time when your best-case scenario crashed into the seemingly worst-case reality? Did you react in a positive or negative way? After the fact, did you begin to see the Romans 8:28 of it all?

11. Sometimes we can't fix our situation, but we can fix our focus. And fixing that focus will help us see the difficult parts of our story from a different perspective. Is there a particular part of your story that you have been looking at through the wrong lens? If so, explain. End today's lesson by praising God for a situation that you've never praised him for before.

Lesson 12

The Perfect Ending to
an Imperfect Story

Most books end with the words THE END. However, this one encourages us to have a new beginning. The final page challenges you to tell your redemptive story with all the broken pieces fitted and fastened together with the golden veins of grace. Let's together look at how we might start doing that.

1. What are ten important truths you have learned from this study that you will apply or have already applied to your life?

2. Going back to lesson 1, are there any chapter titles of your story that you need to change?

3. Draw a timeline of your life, from birth to current day. Mark high spots and low spots along that journey. Note what you learned through each of those memorable moments or chapters.

4. A simple way to engage with others is: (1) ask them their story; (2) tell them your story; (3) share God's gospel story and the impact it had on your life. Take some time to write out God's gospel story so you can be prepared when the time comes. What do we learn about being prepared in 1 Peter 3:15?

5. Let's get out the praise party hats and celebrate! How have your worst chapters now become your greatest victories?

Notes

Chapter 1: May I Please Have a Different Story?

1. Terri St. Cloud, https://www.bonesigharts.com
/store/?search=she+could+never+go+back+and+make+some+of
+the+details+pretty.

Chapter 2: Why Me? Why This? Why Now?

1. Ann Voskamp, *One Thousand Gifts: A Dare to Live Fully Right Where You Are* (Grand Rapids, MI: Zondervan, 2011), 22.

2. Kaylene Radcliff, "A War Story: 'There Is No Pit So Deep God's Love Is Not Deeper Still,'" Christian History Institute, https://christianhistoryinstitute.org/magazine/article/there-is-no-pit-so-deep.

3. "Most American Christians Do Not Believe That Satan or the Holy Spirit Exist," The Barna Group Ltd., April 13, 2009, https://www.barna.com/research/most-american-christians-do-not-believe-that-satan-or-the-holy-spirit-exist/.

4. *Strong's Concordance with Hebrew and Greek Lexicon*, https://biblehub.com/parallel/genesis/1-31.htm.

5. Lysa TerKeurst, *It's Not Supposed to Be This Way* (Nashville, TN: Thomas Nelson, 2018), 24–25.

6. Philip Yancey, Disappointment with God: Three Questions No One Asks Aloud (Grand Rapids, MI: Zondervan, 1988, 1992), 66.

7. C. S. Lewis, *The Weight of Glory* (New York: HarperCollins, 1980), 43.

8. Sermon by Steven Furtick, *I'm Confused About My Calling,* Elevation Church, February 10, 2019, https://elevationchurch.org/sermons/im-confused-about-my-calling/.

Chapter 3: There's Always a Meanwhile

1. Jean-Pierre de Caussade, quoted in *A Guide to Prayer for All God's People*, Rueben Job and Norman Shawchuck, eds. (Nashville, TN: Upper Room, 1990), 244.
2. John Piper, "God Is Always Doing 10,000 Things in Your Life," Desiring God, January 1, 2013, https://www.desiringgod.org/articles/god-is-always-doing-10000-things-in-your-life.
3. Jon Bloom, "When It Seems Like God Did You Wrong," Desiring God, April 25, 2014, https://www.desiringgod.org/articles/when-it-seems-like-god-did-you-wrong.

Chapter 4: The Scab You Won't Stop Picking

1. Alina Tugend, "Praise Is Fleeting, but Brickbats We Recall," New York Times, March 23, 2012, https://www.nytimes.com/2012/03/24/your-money/why-people-remember-negative-events-more-than-positive-ones.html.
2. Lisa Trei, "Women Remember Disturbing Emotional Images More than Men, Study Shows," *Stanford Report*, July 24, 2002, https://news.stanford.edu/news/2002/july24/emotion-724.html. Turhan Canli, John E. Desmond, Zuo Zhao, John D. E. Gabrieli, "Sex Differences in the Neural Basis of Emotional Memories," *Proceedings of the National Academy of Sciences of the United States of America*, vol. 99, issue 16, July 26, 2002, https://www.ncbi.nlm.nih.gov/pmc/articles/PMC125046/.
3. Lawrence O. Richards, *New International Encyclopedia of Bible Words* (Grand Rapids, MI: Zondervan, 1991), 127.
4. Kenneth L. Barker and John R. Kohlenberger III, *Zondervan NIV Bible Commentary, Volume 2: New Testament* (Grand Rapids, MI: Zondervan, 1994), 806.
5. Steven Pressfield, *The Legend of Bagger Vance: A Novel of Golf and the Game of Life* (New York: William Morrow & Co., 1995); *The Legend of Bagger Vance*, directed by Robert Redford (DreamWorks, 2000).

Chapter 5: Changing the Ending to Your Story

1. Bill and Cindy Griffiths, *The Road to Forgiveness* (Nashville, TN: Thomas Nelson, 2001), 14-15.
2. Griffiths, *The Road to Forgiveness*, 10.
3. Griffiths, *The Road to Forgiveness*, 55.
4. Griffiths, *The Road to Forgiveness*, 56.
5. Griffiths, *The Road to Forgiveness*, 56.
6. Griffiths, *The Road to Forgiveness*, 56, 134–35.
7. *"Aphiemi," The Complete Word Study Dictionary: New Testament*, Spiros Zodhiates, ed. (Chattanooga, TN: AMG Publishers, 1992), 229.
8. Brian Zahnd, *UNconditional?* (Lake Mary, FL: Charisma House, 2010), 19.
9. C. S. Lewis, *The Weight of Glory* (New York: HarperCollins, 1949, revised 1980), 182.
10. Brian Zahnd, *UNconditional?*, 10, 12.
11. *"Satam," Strong's Concordance with Hebrew and Greek Lexicon*, Bible Hub (undated), https://biblehub.com/hebrew/7852.htm.
12. *"Parak," Strong's Concordance*, (undated), https://biblehub.com/hebrew/6561.htm.

Chapter 6: Leaving the Shame Place

1. Quoted in Jane Bolton, "What We Get Wrong About Shame," *Psychology Today*, May 18, 2009, https://www.psychologytoday.com/us/blog/your-zesty-self/200905/what-we-get-wrong-about-shame.
2. Brené Brown, *Women and Shame: Reaching Out, Speaking Truths, and Building Connection* (Austin, TX: 3C Press, 2004), 15.
3. *New Bible Dictionary*, 3rd ed., I. Howard Marshall, A. R. Millard, J. I. Packer, D. J. Wiseman, eds. (Downers Grove, IL: InterVarsity Press, 1996).
4. *Webster's Dictionary*, s.v. "shame," www.definitions.net/definition/shame or www.etymonline.com/word/shame.

5. Brené Brown, *Rising Strong: How the Ability to Reset Transforms the Way We Live, Love, Parent, and Lead* (New York: Random House, 2015), 50.

6. Her pastor was right! Pat Layton went on to write a book to help others: *Surrendering the Secret: Bible Study Book for Healing the Heartbreak of Abortion.* To learn more about Pat's ministry, visit her website, patlayton.net.

Chapter 7: When Forgetting Is Not Enough

1. Elisabeth Kubler-Ross, *On Death and Dying,* (New York: Scribner, 1969), ix.

2. Eli Lizorkin-Eyzenberg, "The Incredible Hebrew Blessings for Ephraim," Israel Bible Weekly, July 13, 2020, https://weekly .israelbiblecenter.com/manasseh-ephraim-mean-hebrew/.

3. Lizorkin-Eyzenberg, "The Incredible Hebrew Blessings for Ephraim."

4. Dan Allender, *The Healing Path: How the Hurts in Your Past Can Lead You to a More Abundant Life* (Colorado Springs: WaterBrook, 1999), 151.

5. "Hope," *Baker's Evangelical Dictionary of the Biblical Theology*, Walter A. Elwell, ed. (Grand Rapids, MI: Baker Book House Company, 1996), accessed on biblestudytools.com, https://www.biblestudytools .com/dictionary/hope/.

6. Rubem Alves, *Tomorrow's Child: Imagination, Creativity, and the Rebirth of Culture* (Eugene, OR: Wipf and Stock Publishers, 1972, 2011), 195.

Chapter 8: Why Your Story Matters

1. Rick Warren, *The Purpose Driven Life: What on Earth Am I Here For?* (Grand Rapids: Zondervan, 2002), 290.

2. Levi Lusko, *Through the Eyes of a Lion: Facing Impossible Pain, Finding Incredible Power* (Nashville, TN: Thomas Nelson, 2015), 108.

3. Philip Yancey, *Where Is God When It Hurts?* (Grand Rapids, MI: Zondervan, 1990), 157.

4. Lusko, *Through the Eyes of a Lion*, 108.

Chapter 9: Speaking Up When You Tend to Clam Up

1. Beth Moore, *The Patriarchs: Encountering the God of Abraham, Isaac, and Jacob* (Nashville, TN: Lifeway Press, 2005), 158.

Chapter 10: Disqualified? Says Who?

1. Lysa TerKeurst, *Unglued: Making Wise Choices in the Midst of Raw Emotions* (Grand Rapids, MI: Zondervan, 2012), 33.
2. Seth Godin, "Belief," Seth's Blog, July 29, 2006, sethgodin.typepad .com/seths_blog/2006/07/belief.html.
3. D. L. Moody, quoted in William Backus and Marie Chapian, *Telling Yourself the Truth* (Minneapolis, MN: Bethany House Publishers, 2000), 31.
4. For more biblical truths about who God says you are, see the appendix, "Your True Identity in Christ."

Chapter 11: Lens One or Lens Two? Which Is Better?

1. Steven Furtick, "It's a No Go," Elevation Church sermon, July 29, 2018, https://elevationchurch.org/sermons/its-a-no-go/.

Chapter 12: The Perfect Ending to an Imperfect Story

1. Joni Eareckson Tada, "Foreword: Before You Begin," in Nancy DeMoss Wolgemuth and Robert Wolgemuth, *You Can Trust God to Write Your Story: Embracing the Mysteries of Providence* (Chicago: Moody Press, 2019), 12, 13.

About the Author

Sharon Jaynes has been encouraging and equipping women through ministry for more than twenty-five years. She served as vice president and radio cohost of Proverbs 31 Ministries for ten years and currently writes for their online devotions and First 5 Bible study app. Sharon is also an international conference speaker, author of twenty-four books, and the cofounder of Girlfriends in God, Inc. She and her husband live in Weddington, North Carolina.

To learn more, visit www.sharonjaynes.com or follow her on Facebook at www.facebook.com/sharonjaynes.